FESTIVALS

A SURVIVAL GUIDE

FESTIVALS
A SURVIVAL GUIDE

COPE WITH EVERYTHING:
TENTS • TOILETS • TORRENTIAL RAIN
TOO MUCH BOOZE • AND MORE

DOG 'n' BONE

JO HOARE

Published in 2016 by Dog 'n' Bone Books
An imprint of Ryland Peters & Small Ltd

20–21 Jockey's Fields   341 E 116th St
London WC1R 4BW   New York, NY 10029

www.rylandpeters.com

10 9 8 7 6 5 4 3 2 1

Text © Jo Hoare 2016
Design and illustration
© Dog 'n' Bone Books 2016

A CIP catalog record for this book is
available from the Library of Congress
and the British Library.

ISBN: 978 1 909313 87 3

Printed in China

Designer: Paul Tilby
Illustrator: Paul Parker

Commissioning editor: Pete Jorgensen
Art director: Sally Powell
Production controller: Mai-Ling Collyer
Publishing manager: Penny Craig
Publisher: Cindy Richards

Background images © Getty Images

CONTENTS

INTRODUCTION

Festivals were once little more than people getting off their face in a field, now they're people getting off their face in a field whilst paying as much as they would for a week in Spain for the privilege, but at least they have access to organic falafel burgers and pop-up hair salons.

From being something that marked you out as a bit of a dangerous hippy, festivals are now a bona fide industry with more column inches devoted to the preparation for them than discussions about whether or not Donald Trump's hair is in fact a guinea pig. But what do you really need to know? Well quite a lot actually… rookie mistakes are easy to make if you're a festival virgin but even if you're a seasoned goer, you're always a mere two tequilas away from being the person that passes out in a portable toilet.

Think of your festival as Bear Grylls would an expedition. Identify the risks; ranging from the unthinkable danger of your phone running out of battery to choosing the wrong food when all you have for sanitation is a long drop you're sharing with 60,000 people. Think about the dangerous creatures you're going to meet; do not underestimate the initial threat posed by seemingly innocuous characters like The Princess or The Fancy-dress Douche and pack wisely—a pair of thigh high socks and a can of dry shampoo do not an entire festival kit make. This book will help you with all of the above and if nothing else you could probably get away with using it to bang your tent pegs in…

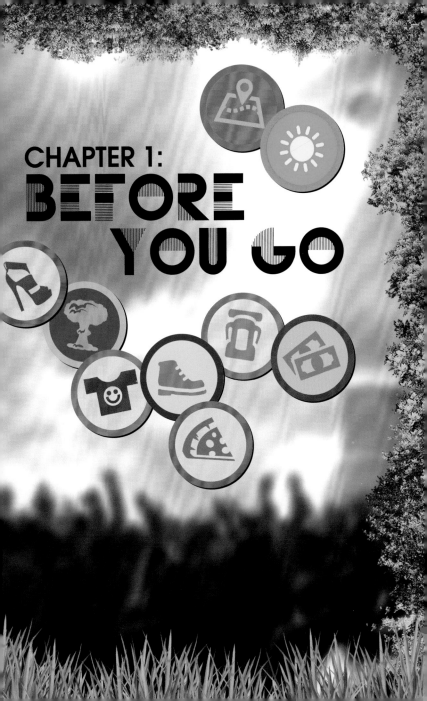

CHAPTER 1:
BEFORE YOU GO

CHOOSING WHERE TO GO

Today's festivalgoers are spoilt for choice. Pretty much any genre you can think of is catered for, often with added extras like comedy stages, gourmet food stalls, spa tents, or whatever pursuits organizers can think up to attract a wider audience. So if you want to spend a weekend camping at the foot of a volcano, listening to punk while getting your nails done and stuffing your face with foie gras there's probably a festival that offers just that. With so much choice how can you pick one that's right for you? Here's a guide to some of the best out there:

NORTH AMERICA

Coachella Despite being known more for the A–Z-list celebrities who turn up each year thanks to its location two hours west of Los Angeles, Coachella always boasts an incredible lineup. Past headliners including Drake, Jack White, Jay-Z, AC/DC, and The Strokes.
Expect desert heat, poseurs, VIP areas, and switched-on music lovers.

South by Southwest Soon to celebrate its 30th year, this festival of music, film, and technology sees over 2,000 acts take to the stage in Austin, Texas. SXSW is THE best festival to catch new bands touted by the music press as "the next big thing." Each night at one of the city's many venues there's a good chance you'll be seeing an act that will be headlining stages across the globe the following year.
Expect people who like to say "I saw them before they were big."

Bonnaroo Not only is this the biggest summer festival in the US, it's also regularly voted the best, thanks to appearances from legends as varied as Willie Nelson, Paul McCartney, Radiohead, and Metallica.
Expect an eclectic lineup appealing to fans of everything from jazz and country to hip hop and metal.

Electric Daisy Carnival For those of you who like your beats repetitive, your clothing neon, and your "drops" bigger than the line for the glowstick stall, this traveling festival showcases the biggest names in EDM music. EDC takes place several times a year at different locations in the US and beyond, with DJs like Tiësto, A-Trak, Skrillex, David Guetta, and Calvin Harris manning the decks.
Expect to be the oldest person there if you're over the age of 23. And to meet a lot of people looking for someone called Molly.

Movement Also known as Detroit Electronic Music Festival, this is the yin to Electric Daisy Carnival's yang. With lineups featuring local techno legends Carl Craig and Kevin Saunderson alongside underground dance music's finest, such as Dixon and Seth Troxler, it's a must visit for electronic music chinstrokers.
Expect lots of serious people talking very seriously about house and techno.

EUROPE

Glastonbury Widely regarded as the best in the world, this is the ultimate bucket-list festival for any music lover. Despite the festival's capacity for over 150,000 people, it's still easier to convince yourself that Kanye West isn't a complete douche bag than to get a ticket. That's no surprise when acts as big as the

Rolling Stones, Bruce Springsteen, Beyoncé, The Who, Arcade Fire, U2, and Stevie Wonder are playing.
Expect rain, mud, hippies, and a mind-blowing amount of things to see and do—from the myriad music stages to the Healing Fields and all-night parties at Shangri-La.

T in the Park Ask many bands where they find the best audiences and there's a good chance they'll say Scotland—the locals love to lose their shit to live music. T provides the perfect excuse to do just that, with artists such as The Libertines, Kasabian, Arctic Monkeys, Noel Gallagher, and Foo Fighters, providing the soundtrack to three days of non-stop revelry.
Expect to go big or go home—don't try to keep up with the locals, they'll drink you under the table.

Sziget Yes, Robbie Williams headlined in 2015, but don't let that put you off. You don't win the award for being the best major festival in Europe by only booking the "fat dancer from Take That," as Noel Gallagher once called RW. Firstly, Sziget's location on the banks of the Danube in Budapest is beautiful. Secondly, artists including Kings of Leon, Major Lazer, Foals, and Placebo should mean you won't find yourself stuck listening to "Angels." Thirdly, there's loads more to the festival than just bands—craft areas, performance arts, and the Chill

Garden beach all provide welcome distractions from Robbie's warbling. **Expect** Take That fans alongside a cool crowd from around the world.

Exit Serbia might not be the first place you think of when it comes to festivals, but since 2000 Exit has been doing an exceptional job of changing that. Last year, nearly 200,000 people headed to the Petrovordian Fortress to experience the atmosphere at one of Europe's most celebrated festivals.
Expect to be amazed at how cheap the beer is and a diverse lineup— Snoop Dogg, Massive Attack, Patti Smith, Guns 'n' Roses, The Chemical Brothers, N.E.R.D., and, er, Gloria Gaynor all played in the last few years.

Croatia OK, this isn't a festival, it's a country, but if you're a fan of dance music you can turn up here almost any week during the summer and find at least one electronic music festival with an idyllic beachside setting. Not only that, many organize amazing boat parties where you can cruise the Adriatic getting off your face to Scuba, Duke Dumont, Jamie Jones, or Erol Alkan. Standouts include Hideout, Outlook, and Dimensions, with each providing a who's who of house and techno.
Expect a party atmosphere with lots of sunburned Brits loving life and listening to the best house, disco, hip hop, and techno.

FURTHER AFIELD

Rock in Rio For reasons beyond us, heavy metal is massive in South America, as evidenced by Rock in Rio, where over 7 million people have attended 16 editions of the festival. The latest saw Metallica, System of a Down, Mötley Crüe, and Slipknot play, but it's not just about metal— Rihanna, Rod Stewart, Katy Perry, and Elton John also shared the bill.
Expect terrified Katy Perry fans accidently ending up in a mosh pit during a set by Korn.

Fuji Rock Festival The biggest festival in Japan also happens to be one of the very best in the world. Despite moving away from its original location at the foot of Mount Fuji, the current site in a ski resort is still awe inspiring, as is the music— OutKast, Arcade Fire, St Vincent, Björk, and Nine Inch Nails all played recently.
Expect to be blown away by how polite the Japanese crowds are— no Bro Pack douchebaggery here.

Splendour in the Grass Australian festivals are in a state of flux, with many boutique festivals adopting a "No Dickheads" policy to put off the idiots who have ruined the vibe at some larger events. Luckily, Splendour remains dickhead-free thanks to a clued-up, music-loving crowd.
Expect arguably the best lineups in Oz: Blur, Mark Ronson, Ryan Adams, Mumford & Sons, and Tame Impala.

GETTING A TICKET

This might sound easy but the difficulty can vary wildly depending on the size and popularity of the festival. At the base level it's like taking candy from a baby, where you substitute "baby" for an adult in a call center or a festival website, "candy" for the ticket, and "taking" for paying legitimately with a credit or debit card to hacking into the mainframe of the Whitehouse (or can anyone do that nowadays with a couple of apps?). At the other end of the scale are those parties that are notoriously hard to buy tickets for, like Glastonbury. For these events you're going to have to work hard and prepare to be disappointed, but the following tips are there to help you increase your chances of securing a ticket. And don't worry if you can't get a ticket for your first-choice festival, there are plenty of smaller ones to go to that are just as fun.

1. WORK AS A TEAM

If the tickets go on sale at a particular time, can a few of you make a pact that the first person to get through on the phone or website buys all the tickets? A word of warning: make sure that you and all your friends are 100 percent committed to going and are prepared to pay for your ticket. Leaving your mate with 10 spare tickets to a Latvian house music three-dayer and two grand on his emergencies-only credit card is not cool.

2. THINK LOCAL

Is there a festival happening near you or one of your nearest or dearest? Or even someone you're neither near or dear to that might owe you a favor? Some festivals offer pre-sale and/or cheaper tickets to nearby residents to make up for the fact their peaceful lives will be shattered for several days by hordes of drunken revellers.

3. TRY TICKET RESALE WEBSITES

If all the tickets have been snapped up through the official channels, it might be worth taking a look at some resale websites. These can sometimes come up trumps BUT beware of dodgy websites and the fact that not all festivals allow for tickets to be sold on. You can't sell or buy tickets on eBay any more but take a look at their sister website, StubHub. Although it tends to advertise tickets at more than face value, the website does at least offer a fan-protection guarantee. Other reputable sites include Viagogo, which only pays sellers after the buyer has received and attended the event, or Seatwave who step in with replacement tickets or a refund should you have any problems. If the tickets on these resale sites are too steep (and they often are), then there are a few smaller direct fan-to-fan websites being set up, which promoters and record companies also allocate tickets to in an effort to stop the huge mark-ups on resold tickets—try Twickets for lots of face value prices.

As a note, tickets that require photo identification, such as

Glastonbury, cannot be bought on these websites. If someone is claiming they can resell such tickets then they are probably fakes, so check that your desired festival definitely allows third-party resale.

4. WORK QUICKLY

Be aware of exactly when tickets come out and how. This will mean signing up to all the newsletters of all the festivals you're interested in attending. As a tip it might be worth setting up a special email address for this because:

a) You'll see it as soon as it comes in because it won't be hidden in a deluge of work emails about not booking the meeting room on the third floor without checking with Sharon and Clare first.

b) You'll be inundated with a load of crap for the next decade because you forgot to tick the "no contact from third parties" box.

Also follow your fave bands and festivals on Twitter/Facebook/Instagram—they might announce early ticket sales as well as run competitions to win places.

5. THINK VIP

The general tickets may be sold out but there are often VIP ones still available. Although these will be more expensive, often they are less than you think and you'll get loads of extra benefits thrown in, like premium parking, nicer camping, and posh toilets.

6. THINK ABOUT THE SPONSORS

When big companies sponsor festivals, they often give their customers a chance to buy tickets first. See if that's the case with any you want to go to.

7. DON'T THINK YOU CAN WING IT AND BUY FROM A SCALPER ON THE DOOR

As soon as you hand your money over to a scalper/tout at the entrance to a festival, that ticket becomes invalid. And be warned that a tout isn't just a sketchy guy in a leather bomber jacket with his hands in his pockets. Anyone at a site who is trying to resell a ticket, even if it's just some poor chap whose mate let him down at the last minute and is just trying to recoup some beer money, will be considered a scalper.

As such, if security or the police spot you, they'll take the ticket off you and refuse you entry. That's if your ticket was even genuine in the first place. Heaps of scalper-sold tickets will be fakes and with entrance staff having all manner of technical wizardry to weed out fraudulent tickets, your crappy, dog-eared, forged-in-someone's-bedroom fake isn't going to fool anyone.

8. USE SOCIAL MEDIA

Put your plea for tickets on social media and get as many of your mates as possible to repost it for you. Scour Twitter using all the hashtags you can think of. Someone always has a friend who has a last-minute holiday/break up/funeral that means they can't, or won't, go any more, which means they'll be looking to get rid of their ticket fast. And if you're the super-spontaneous type this kind of thing often happens just a day or two before the event, so keep looking right up to the last minute.

WHAT TO REALLY PACK

OK, OK, you might think you know what to stick in your backpack, but a quick scan over this checklist will mean you're not going to miss anything of paramount importance or break your back carrying a load of crap you don't need.

WHAT TO PACK

An empty plastic bottle Fill this up from the on-site faucets/taps (make sure you choose the taps that are designated safe for drinking).

A larger empty plastic bottle If you have room in your bag use this to carry water for washing/teeth brushing. If you haven't got room, just be smelly—it won't kill you.

A torch Make sure you bring batteries for it.

Some warm clothes Even if it's boiling during the day, remember it will get cold at night.

Plasters and Band-Aids New boots + being on your feet all day = blisters.

Painkillers You will definitely need these at some point over the weekend.

Any medication you use regularly Asthma inhaler, antihistamines etc. Also, while not strictly medication, be sure to bring contraception.

Sunglasses Essential, not just for sunny days but for epic hangovers too.

A waterproof jacket You'll thank us when it chucks it down with rain solidly for three days.

Toilet roll A no-brainer.

Snacks Cereal bars, potato chips, chocolate bars etc. will give you a bit of extra energy and save you from spending a fortune at the food stalls.

Toiletries Dry shampoo, deodorant, sunscreen, toothpaste, and baby wipes, are all definitely worth packing.

Mouthwash If you really run out of water, it's better than brushing your teeth with beer.

Something to sleep on A camping/exercise mat will do. This is not just for the comfort factor—you'll also be bloody freezing equipped with just a sleeping bag.

An iPad or any other unnecessary tech You can cope without your Apple life-support machine for a few days, right? It'll only get stolen/smashed/soaked anyway.

WHAT NOT TO PACK

Glass bottles Lots of festivals won't let you take glass on site so decant before you go.

Fireworks Sounds like fun but a recipe for disaster. The security staff will have these off you quicker than John Mayer can remove a bra.

Umbrella Everyone will hate you for blocking the view to the stage and some festivals don't allow them.

Too much booze You won't be able to carry all the bottles and if you haven't checked the limits of what you can take in, it may end up getting confiscated.

Selfie sticks You'll look like a chump and probably won't be allowed in with one anyway.

Any clothes you care about There's a good chance clothes won't come back looking the way they did before you left for the festival.

An enormous makeup bag You definitely won't be using those three face serums and four different types of primer.

USING THE TOILETS

Your choice of toilet facilities at a festival can be as varied as the consistency of matter you'll be using them to purge. (If you don't know what we mean by this, then you've never subsisted for three days solely on burgers made from indeterminate meat and Jägermeister.) From the traditional four-walled fume cabinet that is the portable toilet to the eco-friendly long drop, via a journey of multi-opening box urinals and squat-over troughs, there's actually a fair amount of choice when it comes to facilities. While the toilets will never be a highlight of your weekend, if you navigate them with a little forethought then you can stop them ruining your whole festival.

First off, categorize your toilet visits into exactly what you'll be using them for. A quick five-second pee is an altogether different task to that "could be here for some time" tricky first festival bowel movement, so plan ahead.

TAKING A LEAK

Don't hold on until you're REALLY desperate You might think that waiting as long as possible to go means fewer trips, and the desire "not to break the seal" will be strong. The seal theory definitely has some truth to it, but don't leave your toilet visit right 'til the last minute, because you'll forget to factor in the line issue. Those slightly out-of-the-way toilets with next to no line you congratulated yourself on finding a few hours ago? These have suddenly become like that previously undiscovered Greek holiday island paradise—swamped by people and with a Pacha nightclub charging €50 entry. (OK, maybe not the nightclub bit, but you get the metaphorical point about the volume of people.)

Whereas earlier you'd allowed maybe five to ten minutes before your bladder gave way to take a leak, getting to the front of that 100-strong line is now going to take a lot longer. It's worth noting that the pain you'll be in while jiggling from side to side as you count down how long every single bastard in front of you takes to use the toilet, will be nothing compared to the bladder infection you'll be leaving yourself susceptible to should you keep leaving it so long to go.

Do bring your own toilet paper

It will run out. In fact, it's doubtful any ever existed in the first place, which makes toilet paper at a festival as precious a commodity as cigarettes in a prison. Aside from your own needs, if you're the one person in the line with a packet of Kleenex tissues wedged into your bag then expect to make lots of new friends who are all prepared to barter anything from actual money through to drink tokens, smokes, drugs, and maybe even a snog or two.

Don't forget to practice at home if you've bought a ShePee

The ShePee was heralded as the best thing to happen in the field of female public urination since, well, anything really. The part funnel, part faux-penis device claims to fit neatly over the user's crotch, thus sending the flow neatly through a slim chute and enabling women to sort of pee like men. However, users report it's tricky to position, messy, and, unless you're wearing a skirt and no underwear, requires almost total below-the-body disrobing to fit and use. Should that not sound appealing, there are a whole host of other personal devices on the market. These include a camping-

stool commode (basically a canvas chair with a hole cut into it, to which you attach a bag to catch your outgoings), gel-filled disposable urinals, and bottles with unisex attachments to pee into. Whichever method you choose, it's best to have a few trial runs in the comfort of your own bathroom (may we suggest the shower?) before you try whipping it out with a bladder full of Bud in the middle of a field.

Do be considerate OK, you're desperate, but you're not an animal. Boys, that means just 'cos you can pee anywhere doesn't mean you have to. And no, the side of someone's tent is not OK. And members of both sexes, if you're going to attempt to pee in a bottle then dispose of it using a method other than chucking it into the crowd "for a laugh."

Do pack a torch Because nocturnal pees can be disastrous when you can't see where you're going.

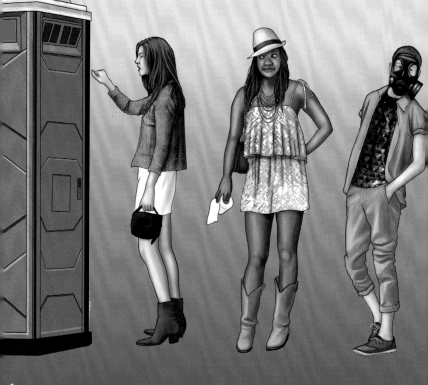

HAVING A CRAP

Do pay for a posh one Nowadays, many festivals have fancy portable toilets, which you can pay to use. The lines are short, the water actually runs, and you'll probably have some dried flowers to look at as you make use of the facilities. This sounds heavenly, BUT don't bother wasting your cash just to take a leak. When the price of a pee costs the same as a beer, you'll be paying as much to excrete your booze as you will be to drink it. However, when the other call of nature makes its voice heard, that is the time to treat yourself to a little comfort. It's also the perfect pit stop to pinch as much toilet paper as you can squeeze in your bag, saving it for when you visit the inevitably paperless plebeian facilities later in the day.

Don't eat anything that might upset your stomach Frankly, it should be illegal to serve spicy food at festivals. As tempting as that extra-hot burrito or lamb bhuna might seem at 2am, remember you won't have the comfort of your own bathroom the next morning.

Do pack Imodium We don't need to tell you why. Should diarrhea strike, and considering the diet, germs, and booze you'll be "enjoying," it's not beyond the realms of possibility that you're going to want to stop it. Fast.

Don't dismiss the long drops Yes, the idea of a long drop is foul and yes, you will lose anything in your back pockets (many is the lighter that met an ugly end here). However, toward the end of a festival the long drop might actually be your best bet for making drop-offs of your own. The thing is, how much fresh air do you think you're going to get in an enclosed box as opposed to somewhere that has an unending supply of odor-free air circulating all around? Worth a try at least.

FESTIVAL FOOD

Long gone are the days of sketchy-looking burger vans, anaemic French fries, and gray hot dogs being all the food options you could get at a festival. Now, we're not saying this food has disappeared because it's still very much alive and kicking at most festivals (barring those that take place in pop-up yurts on rural biodynamic farms where your burger will be made from a cow who lived in a nicer house than you do and was fed solely on Champagne and foie gras), but nowadays there's a much bigger choice of cuisine at even the grubbiest of festivals. Plus, some people even have food as one of their main reasons for going to a particular one—OK, these people are probably your mother and father, but anyway. Having said this, there are still a few things to think about...

1. DON'T PEAK TOO SOON

Yes, that hand-carved hog roast does look delicious, but it's also the same price as three meals at the far more reasonably priced noodle van next door. Budget a little so you don't spend half your cash on your first day. Save your treat meals for later on in the festival when your poor partied-out body will really appreciate the comfort a decent meal brings.

2. DO A LITTLE BIT OF RECONNAISSANCE WORK

Hang out around your chosen food truck for a few minutes to check if the meals doled out actually look like the delicious pictorial depictions. Make sure the huge plate of steaming mac 'n' cheese you thought you were getting doesn't in fact arrive in a bowl so small a kitten would struggle to drink from it. Similarly, if the portions are huge don't order one when you just feel like a snack. Alternatively, share one with a friend.

3. DON'T EAT ANYTHING THAT MIGHT UPSET YOUR STOMACH

Do we really need to point out why?

4. DON'T FORGET TO EAT

Yep, we know that sounds ridiculous, but you'd be surprised how even the biggest of appetites gets dulled by a distorted body clock and a bellyful of beer. Try to remember when it's lunch and dinnertime and take yourself off for something resembling a meal.

5. DO THINK ABOUT HYGIENE

OK, no one's expecting you to lay out a linen tablecloth, but if you're eating with your fingers a quick rub down with some hand sanitizer would be sensible. Also, take a quick look at the stall—is the "chef's" idea of cleaning a saucepan wiping it with the edge of his grubby T-shirt? If so maybe try the next one.

6. DON'T EXPECT TO BE HEALTHY

Don't be that person banging on about quinoa when everyone else wants a bacon sandwich—your diet regime can wait for a few days. You weren't so concerned with what you were putting in your mouth last when you went back to the tent of that guy dressed as Axl Rose, were you?

NOODLE KING

COPING WITH THE WEATHER

Unfortunately, it's fairly common for festivals to be subjected to weather patterns that are more extreme than Donald Trump's latest views on immigration. Whether (sorry) it's the epic rains that regularly turn Glastonbury into a mud bath, the freak winds that forced Benicàssim Festival to completely shut down in 2009, or the sweltering heat that can turn many summer events into a sauna, extreme weather can make a festival feel like a lot of hard work—here's how to survive:

THE RAIN

Heavy rain has been the undoing of many festivalgoers—if the soaked clothes don't get you, the almost ice-like slippery conditions probably will. But the heavens opening doesn't have to mean the end of your fun—there are simple ways to survive it.

1. Stop worrying about what you look like

Swallow your pride and buy a poncho. Yes, you'll look a little like an eight-year-old on a school trip to Disney World, but you'll be warm and dry. And as your mother might say, "This isn't a fashion parade." As a tip, buy one as soon as the rain starts because the wetter it gets the more prices will rise.

2. Pack rubber boots

Your wellies or rubber boots don't have to be fancy ones, but if you think there's even the slightest chance of rain then pack 'em. If nothing else, you can wear them to protect your feet in the toilets. Note: just 'cos you pack a pair doesn't mean you have to use them. Nothing looks more ridiculous than the girl who has perfectly planned her outfit wearing her pink Hunters when there's been a drought warning.

3. Don't go mud diving (at least not on the first day)

As hilarious as an Instagram photo of you swimming in mud will be, can you imagine trying to clean yourself up using only a travel pack of baby wipes? Have you thought about where you'll hang those sodden, stained clothes? If you really must try mud diving, then leave it until the final day when it'll be staff on your train home worrying about cleaning up after you.

4. Think about your phone

If it's tipping it down to the point of everything you own being sodden through, a simple Ziploc bag will ensure your tech doesn't get flooded.

5. Pack some garbage bags and practice good tent wetiquette

Shove wet clothes and boots straight into these bags when you get back to your tent to stop them contaminating your nice dry things. Do remember to pop wet clothes in the wash the instant you get home, before they begin to cultivate hitherto unknown breeds of mildew.

6. Got room for a camping chair?

If things get really muddy, you're not going to have anywhere clean and dry to sit apart from in your tent. Now, that might not sound like much of a big deal, but on day three, when the only time you've not been standing up is while trying to get some sleep, you'll be dead on your feet. A nice, non-muddy sit down will feel like heaven.

7. Remember, the rain will affect walking times

When it's dry and sunny it might take ten minutes to walk between two stages, but add in meters of mud and that time is going to double. As a result, don't cut it fine when planning your route between the bands you want to see.

THE SUN

Yes, the rain is a total pain in the ass, but as idyllic as gorgeous, bright sunshine may sound, this too can cause problems. Actually, a serious case of sunstroke will eff up your weekend far more than a damp sleeping bag.

1. Seek out shade

If you're off to a sunny festival like Benicàssim or Coachella, then getting to the campsite early is even more important. If you can find a scrap of shade then bag it, as sun shining directly onto a nylon tent will quickly turn camping into a boil-in-the-bag experience.

2. Keep your tent cool

Sunlight-reflecting blankets (sometimes called space blankets), similar to those sun reflectors people put in car windows, can be attached to your tent using bulldog clips and will keep off some of the heat. Investing in a cooling spray, or even just a plant mister you can spritz yourself with, will provide temporary relief and is especially good when you've got a tent hangover.

3. Pack sunscreen

Make it a high factor and remember to put it on, especially if you're sweating a lot while dancing. If you think you might forget, try setting an alarm on your phone to remind you to reapply once an hour.

4. Wear a hat

Douse your hat in cold water for a lovely hit of cool. An added bonus is no one will notice your festival hair.

5. Drink lots of water

Make a pact that you'll order a glass of water with every alcoholic drink. Even if you only drink half of it, try to keep your water intake similar to your booze levels. Remember, you'll be losing salt through sweat too, so a salty snack like a packet of potato chips is a good idea.

6. If you suspect someone has sunstroke or heatstroke, take him or her to the medics.

If you or your friend start vomiting, feeling dizzy or confused, or develop an agonizing headache after being in the sun, then it might be time to pay the on-site docs a visit. For less serious cases, sit the affected person in the shade and try to cool down their skin by covering them with a damp towel or sheet. Make sure they drink lots of water.

FESTIVAL FASHION

There are now as many different ways to dress at festivals as there are empty nitrous oxide canisters on the ground. No longer is it enough just to wear what's clean, comfortable, and practical for three days living in a field. If you haven't spent longer planning your look than the acts you're going to see, then you're definitely in the minority... But which tribe to choose? Whichever one you find the least loathsome from the list below.

THE LIFESTYLE BLOGGER

Frankly, it's upsetting enough that being a lifestyle blogger—a role that basically consists of being alive and telling people who don't know you about it on the internet—is now a viable career choice (if your dad owns half of Manhattan). Now, lifestyle bloggers have gone and bloody taken over our festivals. However, there is a fun game to be had at their expense. Welcome to fashion-blogger bingo—score one point for each of the below:

1. Choice of headwear

A black floppy bowler hat. The style worn by the man on the Quaker Oats box is a popular choice.

2. Retro jewelry

This accessory will be worn down to the neck, because the blogger will be embracing "the '90s, guys, 'cos it's just so cute!" She has recently watched a trilogy of throwback Winona Ryder pictures for her #WomanCrushWednesday, so the item in question is one of those stretchy chokers that makes you look like a human Spirograph.

3. Clip-on septum piercing

She bought a multipack in Claire's Accessories. She thinks they make her look like FKA twigs. In reality it's a little more of a bull-being-led-to-market vibe

4. #dungas

A pair of denim dungarees, more suited to someone 38 weeks pregnant or an apprentice garage mechanic than a young woman attending a music event. She will, of course, leave one strap undone, with a neon bandeau from Urban Outfitters worn underneath.

5. Bandanas

Her pockets will be stuffed with multicolored scarves in the manner of a 1970s' homosexual advertising his preferences. Her wrists will also be bedecked, as if she were trying to contain a particularly poisonous snake bite.

6. Doc Martens

Now, these are actually a pretty sensible thing to wear to a festival but she's not wearing them for their practicality, she's wearing them 'cos they make her legs look super skinny in photos.

It's for you if: You start a conversation with a stranger by asking them to guess how many Instagram followers you have.

THE HIPSTER

We are all well versed in the politics of a hipster beard. And as grubby as one is in everyday life (you've seen the articles on Facebook about how they contain more germs than a toilet), can you imagine the filth contained in it when you're not even anywhere near the aforementioned toilet, let alone a shower. The Hipster will also fall foul of festival fashion thanks to his love of exposed ankles. When mud (and worse) reaches up to mid-shin, those natty brogues minus socks aren't going to seem like such a good idea are they?

It's for you if: You still think it's 2012.

THE "AUTHENTIC"

They have only ever bought clothes from stalls at festivals. And that's on the occasions they actually buy them, not "find" them under a pile of comatose teenagers in the corner of a dance tent and discover the unexpected bonus of a baggy in the pocket filled with mystery narcotics. Everything is a muddy color combo that can only be described as Skittle vomit. Everything is unisex and from the pull-on, one-size-fits-all family. Nothing has buttons or poppers or zips. These garments are specifically created to look no better or worse freshly cleaned than they do after being worn for 72 hours straight.

It's for you if: You have no desire to interact with members of the opposite sex. Ever.

THE LITTLE AS POSSIBLE BRIGADE

The origins of the little as possible brigade (AKA the LAPB) are confused. Some might think that wearing only just enough fabric to allow you to evade decency laws dates back to the breast-baring antics of the early days of free love festivals.

Others blame Rihanna; and the fact that every single magazine eulogizes about the fabulous versatility of denim hotpants for your "festival wardrobe." (Note: in this context, versatility relates to the fact that the shorts can give you medical problems ranging from deep chafing to virulent thrush). Origins aside, it's an increasingly popular phenomenon, not just limited to female festival goers, but also with "keerrazzee" types who like to get naked, and pumped-up lads who consider having neon body paint smeared over their torsos and wearing jeans so tight you can identify their religion through them a perfectly acceptable outfit choice.

It's for you if: You don't necessarily see hypothermia as a negative thing. The LAPB devotee is prepared to show 90 percent of their total surface area no matter what the weather.

FASHION DON'TS

ONESIES/JUMPSUITS/DUNGAREES

This one is for both the boys and the girls. Basically, you want to avoid anything that means you have to get naked to pee. Do you want those dunga-straps dangling on the floor of a festival toilet that's been in constant use for three days? How would you feel about your grubby gray bra being revealed to a line of thousands when the dodgy lock on the portable toilet fails and the door swings open? What about a very near miss when a bladder full of three pints of lager has to wait a crucial extra 30 seconds to relieve itself while you work out how to undo the complicated zip on your onesie?

HEELS

Do we need to explain this one? Well, considering it's not an uncommon sight at many festivals then yes, we probably do. You will be walking. A lot. In all kinds of terrain. There will be mud, there will be bloodshed if you stand on anyone's toe, and everyone WILL laugh at you—so don't do it. Also, wedge rubber boots (wellies) are NOT an exception to this rule. They are neither "fun" nor "cute" and will instead make you look like you're wearing 1940s' built-up footwear to correct an unfortunate orthotic issue.

DENIM "UNDERWEAR" AKA HOTPANTS

OK, we know we've got our mom face on here but seriously girls, visible labia should not be the finishing accessory to your look. And you know what short shorts give you (apart from a load of creepy dads taking your picture on their camera phones)? THRUSH. Believe us when we say a hot, sweaty tent is the last place you want your poor bits to be feeling like someone's committed an act of vaginal arson.

OVER-FRINGING

Like the aforementioned dungarees, anything that dangles is a danger. Plus, there's a risk your suedette waistcoat could act like the fuse to a barrel of gunpowder as its tassels trail over the lit cigarettes of your fellow festivalgoers.

A ROCK T-SHIRT OF A BAND YOU DON'T KNOW

"But it looks cool." No it doesn't. If you can't name at least three albums (the band's Greatest Hits collection doesn't count), then you're no better than the guy donning a Ferrari baseball cap to cruise around in his Ford Focus.

FLORAL HEAD GARLANDS

Now more of a festival cliché than making the peace sign in your Instagram photos (stop doing this too, FYI). There needs to be some kind of government intervention to put a stop to flower garlands, because wearing a crown of daisies doesn't make you look free spirited and at one with nature. At best you'll look like a ten-year-old flower girl at a royal wedding and at worst like you've stolen some plastic flowers from a particularly disliked grandma's grave. If you want to announce to the whole crowd that you're the most basic of the basics then go ahead, knock yourself out with a delightful halo of ersatz sunflowers. Do you want to not look like a massive douche? Then leave the faux flowers on the shelf at Claire's Accessories.

SUEDE

Unless you're a Kardashian and throw clothes away once they've come into contact with oxygen for more than 24 hours, then suede at a festival is a no no. Once suede gets dirty, it's dirty for good, so keep that $150 mini skirt for cleaner types of fun.

OVER-THE-KNEE SOCKS

Now, what exactly is the point of these? Surely only unfortunate attendees of British public schools, who were forced to wear shorts even when it was five below think these are a good idea? If it's hot, wear shorts (proper ones mind you, not ones you need a Hollywood wax to even look at); if it's cold, wear jeans. Easy.

SHORTS WHEN IT'S FREEZING

Both sexes fall prey to this and no one quite knows why. Even normally sensible types, who would never leave the house without an umbrella if their iPhone told them there was so much as a five percent chance of rain, abandon all sense of weather sensibilities the moment they arrive at a festival site. Instead, they think that nothing will impede their fun so much as a pair of covered shins. Despite layering up a hypothermia-preventing array of clothing on the top half of their body, nothing will persuade them to give their poor lower limbs a break as they insist (through chattering teeth and blueing thighs) that they're "really quite warm, actually."

MEN IN LOW-CUT V-NECK T-SHIRTS

You will look like a member of a boy band that got knocked out at the judges' houses stage of *The X Factor* and you'll get a really shit tan. This makes wearing one a lose/lose situation.

MEN'S FESTIVAL JEWELRY

Gents, have you bought any of the below specifically to attend a festival? Please tick all that apply:

1) Leather thong bracelets
2) A pendant of anything that resembles a tooth

3) Anything with a peace symbol
4) A neon "friendship" bracelet
5) Dog tags
6) Rosary beads

0 ticks: Congratulations you are not a douche
1–3 ticks: You are a douche
3–5 ticks: You are a massive douche
6 ticks: Burn your festival ticket now. If you go, someone will attempt to assassinate you.

MINI DRESSES

Remember you'll be sitting—most likely cross-legged—on the floor, a lot. Should you wish everyone within a five-meter radius to bear witness to your gusset all day then at least make sure you pack enough clean underwear, hey?

BACKPACKS

Easy to steal from. Also easy to piss off the people behind you when your bag knocks their drinks out of their hands every time you attempt a dance move.

FASHION DOS

Now you know what you can't wear (OK, we're not dictators, maybe we shouldn't use the word can't, lets replace it with: "If you wear any of them then you run the risk of everyone thinking you're a dick/people throwing bottles of piss at you/all your mates refusing to hang around with you), it'd be cruel if we didn't provide you with alternatives. You're welcome.

ACROSS-BODY BAGS

These have all the hands-free capabilities of a backpack with the bonus that you can see exactly what's going on. The truly dedicated can even branch out to a fanny pack/bum bag, but expect to be approached by feverish-looking teens every 15 minutes asking "how much your K's going for?"

SUNGLASSES

Forget these and you'll be at the mercy of the NASDAQ-esque fluctuating prices of the sunglasses stalls. The instant that hangover-worsening sun pokes its head out, the festival becomes a seller's market. This will see you forced to pay a crazy price for a bit of brown plastic that will be about as good for your peepers as a dose of myxomatosis.

SOMETHING WATERPROOF

It's not glamorous or sexy, but a light waterproof jacket with a hood will prove invaluable.

LAYERS

Wear lots of thin layers—think tees, thin jumpers, a vest, a hoody etc. Not only are these much easier to pack, but they're also more versatile than trying to stuff an enormous heavy coat or sweater into your bag.

A HAT

Sun/rain/hiding hair that's greasier than an oil-slicked otter in your Instagram photos… a simple hat works in all situations.

DENIM

It may be a bit of a ball ache to dry, but denim is tough, hard wearing, and easy to wash, making it your festi-fashion best friend.

A BIG SCARF

A thin-but-large scarf squishes down to nothing but has oh so many uses. It's a handy extra layer that you can also use as a picnic rug, or use as a blanket to wrap everyone up in when the sun goes down. Fold it up into a pillow or clip it to your tent to make a sun porch. You could even use it as a sling when your mate slips in a puddle or pile of regurgitated noodles and hurts his arm. The list is endless.

NORMAL RUBBER BOOTS OR WELLIES

The kind you'd wear for a muddy walk; a pair in a plain dark color with no hint of ludicrous "fun" patterns or accessorizing. They are here for function not form, thank you.

CONVERSE

If you are going to a festival with guaranteed sun or are blessed with unseasonably good weather, then you might think flip-flops are a good idea. Think

again. Consider all of the unpleasantness you see (and smell) on the floor at a festival. Now imagine all that grime between your toes and having no means of cleaning between the aforementioned tootsies for three more days. Not to mention the pain that'll occur when at least five festivalgoers a day stomp and stumble on your poor unprotected feet. Put the flip-flops back in your closet and instead pack a lightweight pair of canvas shoes like Converse. Shoes that you can chuck in the washing machine when you get home are perfect.

BIKER BOOTS

For those festivals that are not quite muddy enough for a full rubber boot, but too grotty for Converse (basically every festival ever), biker boots are perfect. For the girls (or boys, if they so desire) these boots are also the perfect accompaniment to dresses and skirts, making your legs look longer and thinner.

CHAPTER 2:
ONCE
YOU'RE
THERE

HOW TO PICK THE PERFECT CAMPING SPOT

Choosing where you're going to set up shop for three days and nights of debauchery isn't always an easy choice. You want to be close enough to the action that you don't have to trudge for miles to get in the mix, but equally you don't want to establish camp right by the speaker stack for the 24-hour dance stage. And don't forget the proximity to the nearest toilets for that inevitable early morning visit. Here are a few bits of advice:

BE REALISTIC

If you like the look of a spot early on in your quest for the perfect pitch, go with your gut instinct. Many revellers give themselves permanent muscle damage lugging a tent, two cases of beer, a gallon of water, and various other essentials around the entire festival site looking for a suitable place to stay. "Let's just go a little bit further," they say as yet another perfectly serviceable pitch is rejected. The chances of getting a quiet, shady spot away from the crowds is about as likely as a snow storm hitting Burning Man festival.

BE NICE

Congratulations, you've got up well before sunrise and have made sure you're one of the first attendees to be let into the festival site. Your reward: the pick of the pitches to camp on. Now don't be an asshole and create your own version of Area 51, cordoning off vast swathes of land so that your mates who are arriving in two days can camp next to you.

This kind of thing is instant bad karma—instead of guarding your pitch like an ornery plantation owner why not go out and have some fun at the festival and let people camp where they want. After all, tents are only for sleeping, you selfish jerk.

A TENT IS GOOD ENOUGH

For some, sleeping in a regular, common or garden tent just isn't an option. "Why sleep under canvas when with just a few planks of wood, a nail gun, cladding, fiberglass insulation, breeze blocks, corrugated iron, a can of paint, a saw, a workbench, some roofing felt, some cement foundations, and a hammer you can create the perfect weekend accommodation." Er, because we're at a festival, not building a romantic cabin in the woods.

STAY AWAY FROM PATHS

Sure, it'll be easier to find your tent, but thousands of drunk people will be marching past your bed throughout the night. Many will be shouting their heads off, making sleep as easy a prospect as blagging your way into the VIP area (see page 68). A lot of people will trip on your guy ropes, making your already precarious dwelling even more in danger of imminent collapse. And there's a fair chance someone will either fall or be pushed into your tent and onto you, snapping the tent poles and making it completely useless. Trust us on this one, it happens.

HOW TO PITCH A TENT

Unless you're one of the chosen few who gets to glamp (see page 110), you're going to need a tent to sleep in. Here are a few things to consider...

DO Spend a bit more than you think you need to. Think of your tent like wine in a restaurant. The cheapest bottle is going to be disgusting. Same goes for the bargain tent. It's going to be a total bastard to put up, will be about as waterproof as a fishing net, and will blow away in wind conditions anyway stronger than a poodle's exhale. If it cost less than $20, it's strictly for kids to use in the back yard. Kids who will then decide to come inside at 10.30pm because it's too cold/full of bogeymen/shit to camp outside when there's a perfectly decent bed and bathroom in the house.

DON'T Forget you're tall, if you're tall. Or fat, if you're fat. The box might say it's a two-man tent, but if you should be more than six foot or wear any clothes larger than size XXL then one size most definitely does not fit all. A three- or four-man version might be a safer option.

DO Make your tent recognizable. You know when you're looking out for your luggage on the carousel at the airport, but everyone has the same black bag and you're damned if you can work out which is yours? Multiply this scenario by 10,000, then swap the bag for a tent—your only source of comfort and shelter having spent 15 hours crushed against sweaty strangers and having walked a marathon trying to find a working toilet or a burger stand that doesn't look like it'll give you dysentery. To make your tent stand out, why not tie your national flag to it. That's if you don't mind people whose sport teams have recently lost to your home nation using the side of your tent as a urinal. For a less inflammatory marker, some ribbon tied through a zip will do just fine.

DON'T Try to pitch a brand-new tent for the first time at the festival. Have a practice run at home and

work out exactly how to put it up. For example, if you've bought a proper tent with guy ropes and pegs then:
a) you're an idiot who should have bought a pop-up tent
b) pack a few extra tools like a mallet to hammer in pegs.
Note: a beer bottle will not work as a makeshift mallet so don't even try.

DO Pay someone else to do it for you. Particularly if you know you're going to turn up late/drunk/are generally pretty useless at this kind of thing. Lots of festivals provide this service—look out for it when you book your tickets—and it's usually not as expensive as you might think. Plus, you'll often get the kind of position that those too tight to pay for such a service could only snag by getting to the festival several days before it starts. Organizers provide and erect (stop sniggering) your tent and you can even pay extra for things like air beds. A further bonus is there's no annoying tent to carry home afterward that's then shoved on top of your kitchen cabinets until it rots into a mildewed heap while you pretend to yourself you're definitely going to use it again someday.

DON'T Get there after the first day (or even on the first day) and expect there to be space anywhere that
a) doesn't have a gradient that would make a perfect side of an equilateral triangle
b) is nearer to the toilets than your toilet brush at home
c) is so far from the main stages that sleeping is rendered entirely un-doable by virtue of the fact that you'll have to set off to trek to the festival site at 4am every day. The early bird catches the worm and all that.

HOW TO STOP LOSING YOUR MATES

Remember when you were little and supermarkets or shopping malls had special meeting points for lost children? A place where kids could wait patiently for parents who had temporarily lost sight of their little darlings while distracted by the cashier's cleavage/ a two-for-one on gin/a fit of narcolepsy due to the fact they haven't had a full night's sleep for seven years? Recently, these places seem to have disappeared (possibly due to the fact that were you to be a local pedophile these spots were as convenient as a McD's drive-thru), but as a fully grown adult you can now repurpose this tactic at the inevitable points over the course of a weekend when all your crowd goes AWOL.

As soon as you enter the main site (when hopefully you'll still be in control of some of your mental faculties/majority of your motor functions), pick an easily recognizable point. You'll need to be pretty specific, so no "somewhere to the right of the main stage" or "round the back of that burger van where we bought those rip-off bottles of water." Once you add 70,000 people into the mix, these vague coordinates will be as helpful as a copy of *Playboy* is to a blind man. Pick something there's only one of; a place that's easy to find, especially as the day goes on and you become less and less compos mentis—by sunset you'll need all the help you can get. If there are fairground rides at your festival (and inevitably there will be, although why anyone would want to further agitate the uneasy blend of greasy festi-food and pints of warm lager already swilling around in the stomach is a mystery), then the tallest one is a good bet. No matter how busy the crowds get, the ride will remain visible. No rides? Choose a point that everyone who works at the festival will be able to direct you to. This will avoid any conversations along the lines of "it's right near Dave's tent. You don't know Dave? The big guy with a skinhead?" Instead, think first-aid tent, specific numeric gate, or the VIP entrance.

Now, as well planned as your meeting point might be, what if you're the only one lost and your friends simply couldn't give a crap about finding you and have forgotten you exist? In this situation you could be waiting at that meeting point until you're chucked out at the end of the festival along with the abandoned tents and plastic bags full of human excrement. What then? Definitely do not think you'll be able to rely on your phone… "Oh, I'll just find them using location services; I downloaded that handy Find-a-Friend app; I'll send a group WhatsApp dropped pin; hell, I'll just go old school and call them…" No, no, and no again. Newsflash: fields are not good places for phone reception at the best of times, let alone when the number of people trying to get through to their mates to

tell them they've just taken a leak next to a D-list celebrity is equivalent to the population of a small city.

If you're the lost one and the meeting point strategy is a non-starter, the best thing to do is just to embrace it. Go see the bands you want to see, eat the food you want to eat when you want to eat it, and hang out by yourself. You might even make some shiny new friends who are way better than those losers you came with.

DEALING WITH A FRIEND WHO'S PARTIED TOO HARD

Whether it's that last Jägerbomb or that hash none of you were quite sure about, there's always bound to be one casualty on at least one night of a festival and it could easily be you. Here's how to deal with it...

DO Plan ahead. Before you imbibe/ingest whatever it is that you're planning to get off your face on, make sure you have some idea of the set-up of the festival. Do you know where your tent is in relation to the stages? Have you arranged a meeting place (see page 44)? Do you all have enough money on you to buy some water and food? Make sure your mates know what you're taking. If you end up with the medics, it'll be a lot better if they know what they're dealing with.

DON'T Be afraid to call the experts. All festivals have medical tents, make sure you know where these are and if your friend is in real trouble get them there as soon as possible. Don't be worried that staff will think you're being over the top, they won't. Remember, there's probably been a

girl in there crying minutes before because her new boots have given her a sweat rash, which she's mistaken for meningitis. Also, if your friend's situation is due to something a little less legal than a white-wine spritzer, don't be worried that you'll be getting your mate in trouble. Medics see this situation all the time and are not going to tell the police/get you chucked out of the festival/phone your parents. They're just there to look after everyone.

DON'T Leave your friend on his own. Yes, it's annoying as hell that he's chosen five minutes into the set of your favorite band to selfishly collapse, but come on—this is your friend! If you suspect it's nothing more than a few too many Smirnoff Ices, try to get some water and carbs down him, then see if you can help him walk off a bit of the booze. Do not let him stumble back to the tent on his own as he'll have a 0.1 percent chance of making it.

DO Keep an eye on your friend through the night. Tempting as it may be to put your mate in your tent, then bunk up in another friend's tent to avoid the snoring/risk of vomiting, the wise thing to do is to stay with them. If they are really hammered and someone knows the recovery position (look it up now), then it's a good idea to use it on their snoring body. That way if they are sick in the night it'll be the sleeping bag, not their lungs, that suffers. Alternatively, put them on their side with something behind to support their back—a backpack will do. This should stop them rolling onto their back.

DO Leave the casualty with supplies. Placing a bottle of water or a sports drink and a painkiller or two within reaching distance will earmark you as their best friend for life.

DON'T Get angry. The next morning is the time to give them a harsh dressing down/make them pay for all your drinks. Shouting at your friend when they're totally wasted will just escalate the situation.

GETTING BOOZE PAST SECURITY

The policies and policing of taking in "alcohol not purchased on the premises" vary from festival to festival. If you find yourself attending one where the restrictions on liquids are on a par with the treatment your bag might get at JFK airport were you to be on Interpol's most wanted list, then you'll need to get creative.

Now, you might just think, "Screw it, I can't be bothered to carry my own booze anyway, I'll just buy it when I'm in there." STOP RIGHT HERE. Even if you're Prince Harry (we'll presume you're not) and can afford to spend the GDP of a minor nation on a three-day supply of lukewarm lager, it's the queue factor rather than cost that'll ruin your weekend. Like a horrendous math equation, you'll soon find that time lining up for beer becomes equal to the need to pee. As such, you will bounce from bar to bathroom line all day, before seriously considering using your battered plastic pint glass as a receptacle for both. So, swallow your pride (but not your concealed booze, don't take a leaf out of the drug smuggler's handbook—condoms full of gin won't work) and learn to cheat the system.

1. MAKE LIKE THE PERU TWO

No, we're not suggesting you put your hair into a giant donut bun to emulate the smuggling MO of the now infamous Brit drug mules, but there might be something in emulating their food-based method of concealment. Yes, the two girls were discovered, but we're going to hazard a guess that the security at your chosen festival is a little less thorough than at customs on major drug-smuggling routes. For example, Pringles cans can work a treat for slim bottles (hint: go plastic so the weight isn't instantly a giveaway), just leave a few chips on top should any nosy guards try to "pop."

2. DON'T FORGET YOUR SUNSCREEN

If you can be bothered, thoroughly wash out a sunscreen bottle and fill it with booze. If washing sounds like too much effort, or you want to add an extra level of concealment (and you're sensible with your SPF), then leave a little cream in the bottle and instead push in a freezer bag, which you can then fill with contraband and tie before poking it to the bottom.

3. BREAST ENLARGEMENT

With some push-'em-up bras containing more fluid than a hippo with severe water retention, it's perfectly conceivable that your cleavage will be a little squishy. Fill a few freezer bags with your spirit of choice and stuff them into the bottom and sides of a bra that's too big.

4. SPORTY SPICE

Know someone that does triathlons? Well, the point of your friendship is about to become apparent (all those years of sponsorship and listening to them drone on about transition times have got to be worth something, right?). Chances are they'll have a CamelBak, which, for the uninitiated, is like a skinny backpack crossed with one of those comedy hats with straws that you attach two beer cans to. Fill with booze, put on under a sweater, then under your regular backpack and no one will be any the wiser.

5. MINI BAR

Slim of leg? Turn your rubber boots (wellies) into a mobile mini bar by stuffing small bottles of wine down the sides. Admittedly they won't be the coldest drinks you've ever had but that's a small price to pay.

6. IF YOU'RE REALLY DESPERATE…

You can get your hands on various "comedy" hip flasks in the shape of hairbrushes, lipsticks, etc., but the paltry amount of alcohol you'll be able to secrete in one won't even save you enough cash to cover the cost of buying it in the first place. If you're totally shameless, go medical. Order yourself a colostomy bag, no bruiser on minimum wage is going to risk a closer look at that.

COPING WITH A HANGOVER

Now, the morning after the night before is tough enough when you've got ready access to a comfy bed to curl up in/privacy of your own toilet to hug/inexhaustible access to fresh cold water/a full "to watch" list on Netflix/a whole medicine cabinet to raid. When you're clammy and nauseous at a festival, with little more in the way of home comforts than a squashed toilet roll for a pillow and a half-full bottle of Coke that you're 90 percent sure no one's used as an ashtray, hangover recovery can be hard. Here's how to do it like a pro:

REHYDRATION MEDS ARE A GODSEND

Junior doctors sort their hangovers in a hurry with an IV drip. Now, even if you were to be medically trained, a grubby tent is not the most hygienic of places to be replenishing lost vitamins intravenously, so make sure you pack the next best thing. You may have a packet of rehydration salts like Dioralyte laying around from that bout of holiday tummy in Mexico. Take the box and shove it somewhere easy to find in your backpack and try to drink a sachet before you go to bed. (And yes we realize that "bed" is being used in the loosest sense of the word here, but back seat of stranger's car/ overlooked corner of the dance tent/ underneath a hedge all count.) Drink another sachet as soon as you wake up, it will help. If you're organized, pre-mix it in a bottle with some water and sleep with it next to you.

DON'T OVERDO THE ENERGY DRINKS

Sure, they'll give you a quick hit of energy, fooling you into thinking you're OK, but the caffeine-induced crash that'll come after just isn't worth it. Try a sports drink like Gatorade or Lucozade instead.

GET OUTSIDE

Or at least get some fresh air into your tent. Sweltering in the fug of your own (and your possible tent buddy's) sweated-out booze can only be making you worse. Drag yourself outside (even if it's raining) and we guarantee you'll feel an improvement.

AVOID THE TOILETS

Festival toilets are the last place you want to be retching on your hands and knees. If you think you're going to be sick, take yourself off to a quiet little corner of the field. Bring a water bottle with you to considerately swill your vomit away.

PACK SOME BANANAS

When you can face it there will be a plethora of greasy breakfast stuff available on site (eggs are your best bet), but until you can begin to contemplate dragging yourself to a stall then the potassium hit of a banana should help you to feel better.

COPING WITHOUT A SHOWER

To be honest, being gross and grubby is kind of the point at festivals, but if you're really worried about the thought of abandoning all hygiene, there are a few things you can do to make it a little more bearable.

BABY WIPES ARE YOUR BUDDY

Use them once or twice a day for a quick freshen up of all the bits you think need it. (Clue: back in the day this used to be called a whore's bath, in case you weren't sure which areas you should be paying attention to.) Don't use wipes on your face if you've got sensitive skin and/or are prone to breakouts (and keep away from your eyes full stop), because, despite the fact their usual purpose is wiping crap from a delicate newborn's behind, they can still cause irritations. Buy a mini pack of facial cleansing wipes instead, which won't take up any room in your backpack.

PACK HAND SANITIZER

And use it. Doing without running water for a shower might just make you a bit sticky and smelly, but doing without it after using a portable toilet could mean getting a nasty bout of gastroenteritis.

SOUNDS OBVIOUS, BUT START WITH A CLEAN SLATE

That means showering and hair washing as close to the moment you leave for the festival as you can. Also, make sure all your clothes are freshly washed and that any bedding, sleeping bags, etc. are as clean and aired as possible.

TRY TO KEEP YOUR TENT AS CLEAN AS YOU CAN

This will help you to stay cleaner, too. That means don't eat smelly foods inside and leave muddy boots outside.

TAKE FLIP-FLOPS IF YOU'RE CONSIDERING BRAVING THE ON SITE SHOWERS

There will be one hell of a line to use them and neither the water pressure nor temperature will be what you'll regard as luxurious. But these are minor inconveniences compared to the possibility of walking away with a foot full of veruccas or nasty case of athlete's foot. Trying the showers at non-peak times is also a good tip, so avoid them first thing in the morning and instead try when there's a big band on that you're not that bothered about seeing but everyone else is.

TAKE A BIG BOTTLE OF CHEAP SUPERMARKET WATER FOR TEETH BRUSHING

Small bottles of water on site can cost a bomb and no one wants to spend $4 a day on something they spit out onto the ground.

PACK AN EMPTY CONTAINER YOU CAN FILL FROM ON SITE WATER TAPS

Use these to give your face/head a quick rinse. You'll be amazed at how much fresher it makes you feel.

DON'T FREAK OUT ABOUT DIRTY HAIR—YOU DO HAVE OPTIONS

If you really can't do without washing your hair, try dry shampoo in the first instance. Still feel you need a full hair wash? You could invest in a solar shower. This is basically like a medical drip, but it's full of water, not something icky like blood or saline. You hang it from somewhere—top of your tent/willing friend's arm etc.—and it'll trickle down over you. The fringe wash is another popular festival trick and you can do it over a sink or with a bucket, just shampoo the front section of your hair and you'll easily get another day or two of respite. If that sounds too much like hard work and you've got some cash to spare, many festivals now have some kind of "salon" where, for the cost of a few beers, you can get a full hair wash and even a blow dry or fancy up do. Hardened festivalgoers may scorn you, but if you've got your sights set on some festi-sex (see page 54) then it'll be money well spent.

ESSENCES

SHAMPOO
MINT

HAVING SEX IN A TENT

So, festivals are supposed to be all about sex, drugs, and rock 'n' roll. Now, if you're firmly ensconced in either of the latter then the former is going to be a breeze 'cos you're going to be a) so wasted you care not for the (im)practicalities of in-tent intercourse, or b) in a cozy VIP Winnebago situation that's probably comfier than 99 percent of the beds you've already had sex in. However, should you not be heavily chemically assisted and/or headlining the Main Stage then getting it on when all that's separating you from the outside world is a bit of flimsy plastic takes a bit more thought.

1. PLAY SAFE

Obviously, if you're indulging in a bit of "stranger danger" and picking up someone new then it goes without saying that your rain boots shouldn't be the only rubber you're pulling on. Even if you're getting festi-frisky with your significant other, bagging it up means no one gets the soggy side of the sleeping bag. Maybe avoid a novelty glow-in-the-dark prophylactic though. No one wants to create a human zoetrope with their penis after all.

2. DON'T BE TOO AMBITIOUS

Be realistic. You have approximately four feet of space per person in this field and, due to your bad positioning/poor tent purchasing skills, it's impossible to lie at anything other than a badly drawn right angle. Due to space restriction, a marathon multi-position session is going to result in, at best, some guy rope flaccidity (not a euphemism) and, at worst, matching hernias. Stick to spooning, hey?

3. POOR PREPARATION RESULTS IN POOR PERFORMANCE

There's no such thing as successful spontaneous sex at a festival. You need to have ensured the only thing digging awkwardly into your back is your new buddy saying good morning, not the edges of huge rocks you couldn't be bothered to move before you proceeded with erection (pun intended.) Take a few minutes to stamp down uncomfortable mounds of earth and kick away spiky pebbles and stones.

4. THINK CLEAN

With the lack of washing facilities we don't need to spell out the reasons why it might be best to try to make your festival conquest on the first or second night.

5. EVERYBODY NEEDS GOOD NEIGHBORS

Have some consideration for the fact that a tent is essentially as soundproof as a sheet of tissue paper. Try to stifle those multi-orgasmic cries. Everyone outside will just assume you're faking anyway.

HOW TO SLEEP

OK, no one goes to a festival with the aim of getting the usual eight hours of sleep a night, but no shut eye at all makes for a very miserable time indeed. You're going to need to get a few Zs in you—here's how to give yourself a fighting chance.

1. PACK AN EYE MASK

Away from the luxury of curtains and blinds, it's easy to forget that in the height of summer the sun can come up as early as 4am. In other words, about half an hour after you've made it to bed. And tents are not well known for their blackout qualities.

2. DON'T PITCH YOUR TENT IN TRAFFIC

Avoid putting your tent too near a walkway or toilet. People will constantly be walking backward and forward past you and they won't be considerate about noise.

3. TAKE EARPLUGS

There are heaps of different types— from the foam freebies you get on flights to the huge ear defenders Apple Martin wears backstage—but not all work for everyone, so be sure to try them out at home before you go. You won't be quite so smug when your carefully packed pair does absolutely eff all.

4. TAKE NAPS

If there's no one you want to see mid-afternoon, then take advantage of what should be a relatively quiet time at your campsite and slot in a siesta.

5. INVEST IN SOME HOME COMFORTS

An air mattress here or pillow from home there will make all the difference. Haven't got room for a proper pillow? Then take a pillowcase and stuff it with clothes for a makeshift headrest.

6. CONSIDER GLAMPING

Yes, it sounds twattish (see page 110), but if you're the kind of person whose weekend will be ruined if you can't sleep, then the comfort of a glamping yurt, pod etc. really does make a difference. Plus, it's not always as expensive as you think.

7. BRING PJS

By PJs we don't mean that Hello Kitty nightie with the hugging cats, but instead something cozy, comfortable, and warm that will withstand a nocturnal dash to the toilet. Jogging bottoms or sweatpants and a T-shirt are perfect, because trying to sleep in filthy jeans and a damp hoody is never gonna work.

MANAGING YOUR PHONE

OK, we know that years ago people didn't have so much as a pair of shoes at festivals, let alone a $500 mini computer to worry about. Today, because most of us can't last five minutes without checking for messages, phones have become a huge part of the festival experience. As such, it's important that you think ahead a little if you know you're going to be relying on yours.

MAKE IT SAFE

At a festival, there are two dangers for your phone and they are called "you" and "everybody else." Falling under the "you" category is general loss, damage, and idiocy. The main worry for "everybody else" is the growing number of people turning up at festivals with the unadulterated aim of stealing your stuff. Here's how to minimize the risks of both…

YOU

Loss Firstly, set up a PIN or password. Lost phones do actually get handed in. At Glastonbury last year 118 handsets were passed over to organizers to reunite with owners. Having the PIN or passcode is the quickest way to prove a lost phone is yours. Not to mention, if you do lose a phone the PIN will ensure no one's going to be able to see those ill-advised tent nudes you took last night. Another good idea is to activate phone tracking before you go. Career crims will be able to disable this, but if the phone's just fallen out of your pocket then you have a decent chance of being able to find it.

If you're going in a group and you're REALLY organized, a good tip is for you all to have a root round for an old phone—you'll most likely have one hiding somewhere in a drawer. Buy a cheap pay-as-you-go SIM card for the handset (you can get one for the cost of a festival beer or two) and keep it as a backup phone in case anyone in your group loses theirs.

Damage If you do nothing else, get yourself a case. Depending on your level of clumsiness and/or incompetence, you can buy one ranging from a basic bit of extra protection should you drop it/sit on it/mistake it for a Frisbee all the way up to the kind of all-eventuality, waterproof, military-esque cover that even Bear Grylls might consider a bit OTT.

Idiocy If you're prone to being a moron then there's not much we can do to help you, but here are a few common, easy-to-avoid idiotic mistakes.

Don't Use it anywhere near the vicinity of a toilet. The story about the girl diving into the portable toilet to retrieve her phone and getting sucked in is sadly not an urban myth (see page 116).

Don't Lend it to someone you've just met, even if they are "really hot."

Don't Use a charging point if it looks dodgy. Is there some bloke with a cardboard sign saying "Charg Ur Fone Here" and an extension cable that doesn't seem to plug in anywhere? He's probably not legit.

GET CHARGED

OK, so electricity at a festival is rarer than toilet paper, but there are a few ways to get some energy:

★ Think about investing in a portable charger, but remember these need to be fully charged themselves before you can use one, so be sure do it before you go. You could even double-up with a case charger.

★ If you or any of your friends drive to the site, be sure to take an in-car charger. The car will need to be on so it's unlikely you'll have enough time to get a full charge (unless you want to risk running the car battery all the way down), but 5 or 10 minutes will get you some extra juice in an emergency.

★ Make use of official charging stations, but be prepared to pay a pretty hefty fee for the privilege.

EVERYBODY ELSE

Theft There's no point in pretending theft isn't a problem at festivals. That cocktail of drunk punters, the fact we all now carry easy-to-swipe tech worth a small fortune around with us, and the poor security offered by a zipped-up canvas bag mean it's super-easy pickings for unscrupulous bastards. Having said that, there are a few things you can do to lessen your chances of becoming a victim.

Don't Lock your tent. Yes, this sounds weird, but nothing screams "SWAG IN HERE!" like a hefty padlock on a tent zipper. Plus, as a method of protection it's about as effective as the withdrawal method. All it takes is a quick slash with a pair of scissors/knife/spiky heel of a shoe and the thief has created another entrance for himself (and totally ruined your sleeping space into the bargain). A far better idea is just not to bring anything that you'd really be bothered about if it went AWOL, and to keep your valuables on you at all times.

Don't Keep getting your phone out when you're hammered. Checking Facebook, looking at the time, checking Facebook again, wondering if you might have suddenly managed to unearth a local farmer's Wi-Fi and be able to hack into it… Every time you do this you're showing any beady-eyed thieves exactly where you're putting that phone and they're working out a plan to liberate it. Will it be the accidental stumble that results in it being lifted from your baggy jacket pocket or the swipe from the easy-to-access unzipped bag?

Do Sort some insurance before you go and make sure it covers you at a festival.

Do Make sure you know your phone's EMEI number before you go. It'll be on the side of the box the phone came in or look up your model online and there's usually a code you can type in to find it out. The police will often ask for this when you report a stolen phone.

Do Back up all important pictures, videos, and contacts before you go. We're not saying you're DEFINITELY going to lose your phone, but better to be safe than sorry.

HOW TO STOP YOUR BATTERY FROM RUNNING DOWN SO FAST

Rather than spend hours either in a line for a power point or trudging to your friend's car to charge your phone, the best thing you can do is try to conserve your battery. Most of these tips relate to an iPhone, so sorry if you're one of those tech heads who insist that Android phones are far superior. Most people have just got Apple phones, OK?

Turn down the screen brightness
Most of us have it cranked up high so we can use it as a torch in the middle of the night when we want a pee without having to turn on the light, but you're going to have to compromise on your nocturnal urination (just pack a torch, hey?). Simply turn the brightness as low as you can get away with will make your battery last a whole lot longer. Also, make sure you have auto-brightness turned on; it'll dim the screen automatically.

Remember to close your apps
Hardly anyone actually does this, we just minimize them. Double tap your home button then flick up each open app to close it. You'll be amazed that the Dominos Pizza app you once tried to use drunkenly three months ago is probably still running and feasting on your battery life.

Turn off your Wi-Fi
Like an exhausted lothario prowling the club at 2am for anyone to share a lights-up snog with, your phone is constantly on the lookout for connections. This drains the battery like no one's business.

Turn on airplane mode
Obviously you won't be able to text, make calls etc., but you'll still be able to do more than if it was turned off. Here's a practical tip: screenshot useful things like a map of the festival site or details of who is playing where and when so you can look at it offline. If you do manage to find any kind of charging point, switch the phone to airplane mode then too as it'll charge much faster.

Turn off location services
Sorry Tinder, but you're unlikely to work in a field anyway.

Switch off any kind of vibrating alert
This should be a no-brainer.

Keep an eye on how many pictures you're taking
Do you need seventeen different selfies in front of the so-far-away-they-could-be-anyone stage? Doubtful. And be sure not to use a flash when it's not needed.

Switch off emails
We're pretty sure you can do without knowing that Jan from Accounts' leaving card has gone missing.

Ration your online time
Do you really need to check your Instagram again to see if you've got the magic 11 likes yet?

Keep your cool
High temperatures drain the battery, so keep it out of the sun (if you're lucky enough to get any).

HOW TO AVOID SPENDING A FORTUNE

Festivals these days aren't cheap and the chances are the cost of your ticket has already meant forsaking a summer vacation/dinner for the last three months/those books you really should have bought for your college degree. Before you have to sell a kidney to fund your weekend away, let's try to help you rein in your spending a little with a few simple ways to save you some extra cash.

BOOK YOUR JOURNEY IN ADVANCE

This is a key consideration because it can add a significant amount to your festival costs. However you plan on getting to the festival—whether it's train, bus, plane, or car—and however far you'll be going, it's sure to be cheaper if you arrange your travel plans as soon as you've booked your festival tickets. Don't forget to research travel costs before committing to going. That bargain weekend festival in the middle of nowhere might not be such a good deal when you add in the fact you've got to spend double the cost of the ticket price to take a taxi for the last leg of the journey.

GETTING THERE

Are you planning on driving? If so think about car sharing to cut fuel costs. Lots of festivals have a forum on their website where you can find out about this.

SET A DAILY BUDGET

OK, this does sound dull but try it— this is especially important if you're going away for anything longer than a weekend. No one wants to go crazy on the first day of a five-day party, then spend the rest of the time sipping water and considering eating a plate of food you've seen someone discard on the floor.

ATMS

Make sure you withdraw some money before you go. Most cash machines on site will charge you an extortionate fee to use them. Plus, the queues are always ridiculous, particularly on the last day of the festival.

WATCH OUT FOR THE MERCHANDISE

When you are dizzy and excited about the amazing band you've just seen on the Main Stage, the temptation to run straight over to the nearest merchandise stall and snap up a T-shirt/bumper sticker/temporary tattoo of your new favorite act can be too great to resist. Before you spunk all your hard-earned cash on a hoodie you'll probably never wear again, give yourself a little cooling-off period. If you're still desperate to own that tee/sticker/tatt in the morning, you can always come back for it.

THINK ABOUT VOLUNTEERING

Yes, you might have to clear away a tent filled with human feces (this actually happened at Glastonbury one year), but volunteers get free entry, accommodation, and meals, and you won't be working constantly so will have free time to enjoy the festival.

FIND OUT WHAT THE TAKE-IN BOOZE LIMITS ARE

All festivals operate different policies on booze, so it's definitely worth checking the deal beforehand. Some will let you take alcohol wherever you like, some allow cans and plastic bottles in the camping area only, while others don't allow any alcohol at all. If you can bring your own, then obviously you want to take enough alcohol to last the weekend, but imagine the heartache if you're over the limit and your entire stash is chucked away ("repurposed" by the security staff) at the entrance.

DON'T BUY OFFICIAL LANYARDS/MAPS/GUIDES ETC

All the necessary information will be available online before, for free. Buying a guide will mark you out as a total festival novice and be a waste of cash. Just print off anything that looks useful and take it with you.

SAVE YOUR CUPS

Lots of festival bars offer a financial incentive for bringing your old cups back to be reused/recycled. It might only be small change each time, but over the course of a weekend that soon adds up.

EATING

Take some food with you. A few basics like cereal bars, crackers, some Pringles, or nuts and fruit means you can skip a few paid-for meals. When you're spending the same price for a reconstituted horse burger as you would for a meal at a decent restaurant that saving adds up quickly. Also, choose the food you buy wisely—suss out the vans and stalls that give mega-sized portions and you can split one with a mate.

GETTING TO SEE ALL THE BANDS YOU WANT TO SEE

Chances are there will be a couple of acts on the festival lineup that made you decide to part with your cash and give up all your home comforts for a few days. Given the fact that you've gone to so much time, effort, and sleep deprivation to be at the festival, you'd quite like to catch a few of their songs. However, if this is your first festival you might find that watching your favorite bands is not quite as simple as it sounds. Here's how to make it easier:

USE THE INTERNET TO YOUR ADVANTAGE

Try looking at a website like Clashfinder General. Here you can organize and print your dream schedule before you go. Note that we say dream schedule, 'cos, you know, life gets in the way and that toilet queue/hot girl/hangover/overly energetic security guard can all have an impact on the best-laid plans. Prioritize the artists you really want to see and then leave a bit of it to chance—you might discover some music you love that you've never heard before. If you do stumble across a new act, then try the three-track rule—if you're not into them after three songs, then get moving.

BE INDEPENDENT

Don't be afraid to go off on your own to see a band. If all your mates are heading to the Dance Tent and one of the artists you most wanted to see is on the Main Stage, then be brave and go off on your own. (The only exception to this is if you're totally wasted, then you should stick to safety in numbers.) There's a good chance you'll make friends in the crowd and they might even be more fun/better looking than the gang you arrived with.

IT'S NOT JUST ABOUT THE MUSIC

Be sure to leave yourself some time just to wander around the festival. There will be a lot of non-musical stuff going on—from wedding chapels and mindfulness workshops to face painting or simply excellent spots for people watching. If it was only bands you wanted to see, you'd be better off at a gig.

LEAVE PLENTY OF TIME TO GET BETWEEN STAGES

Don't forget that weather/that cute guy in the queue at the bar/60,000 other people will add time to your carefully planned schedule. That walk in the sunshine from the World Stage to the Indie tent that took ten minutes before breakfast this morning will become a lot harder to navigate once the other 59,999 people wake from their tents. As a rough guide, allow triple the time it took to be really sure you'll get to watch a band you really want to see.

TAKE A WATCH WITH YOU

Have a way of telling the time other than your phone, because your battery will definitely die. Also, don't rely on keeping your schedule on your phone for the same reason, a quickly printed-out copy or lanyard from the site will prove invaluable.

GETTING INTO THE VIP AREA

First off, make sure it's a VIP area actually worth trying to sneak into; lots of festivals now offer a "VIP" experience where you'll pay a bit extra on your ticket in order to gain access to a slightly different part of a field that has marginally fewer queues and a slightly less dysentery-provoking choice of bathroom. If you make the effort to scam your way into here, then you're going to be sorely disappointed when there's not so much as a free half pint of beer on offer. However, gain entry into the genuine VIP area and you'll discover everything from a completely free bar and complimentary delicious meals to hair salons and hot tubs—you've reached festival nirvana. Gaining access is not the easiest thing to do but it's worth a try. Here are ways to boost your chances of success:

1. ACT LIKE YOU BELONG

Find the VIP entrance and work out the method to gain entry. Is it as simple as just flashing a wristband or giving a name on a guest list, or are they doing something more complicated like scanning a ticket? If it's the wristband flash, then see if you can find anything that's a similar color to that day's exclusive wristband—a wide hair tie, some ribbon, a strip of paper etc. Fix this to your wrist then dart past security holding your faux-wristbanded arm up as you hustle through in an important fashion. It's worth trying this tactic even if you can't get your hands on something to make a DIY wristband. Just hold your arm high, keep your head down, and if the guards aren't looking that closely you may be lucky.

2. WORK ALONE

Or with one other person. Trying to smuggle in a large group is nigh on impossible.

3. BE REALLY NICE TO SECURITY

Not that nice (we're not expecting you to prostitute yourself), but in a sea of drunk, entitled assholes a polite smile and maybe even a teeny-tiny bribe of a fresh bottle of water or a newly purchased burger handed over to hungry security guards unable to leave their station might just do the trick.

4. LOOK USEFUL

Similar to carrying a watermelon, if you can find a box, then make out like it's weighing you down and claim it's the special vodka/green M&Ms/Chihuahua that the headliner has requested. Stress that you've got to deliver it backstage or otherwise Dan (there's ALWAYS a Dan) is gonna go mental.

5. HANG AROUND OUTSIDE

The VIP area will be full of corporate invites and people associated with specific acts. This means a number of people who may very well only be attending for a few hours before heading home. If they're feeling generous, they might peel off their AAA sticker or wristband and hand it over to you.

VODKA

6. PRETEND YOU'RE A CELEBRITY

Do it with enough confidence and pick the right celeb—the drummer in a relatively obscure band performing on the New Bands Stage is more believable than trying to convince people you're Kanye West. A hoodie and a record bag is an effective standby for pretending you're a DJ—no one ever knows what they really look like anyway.

7. ZIP YOURSELF INTO A BACKPACK

You might laugh but that's how one festivalgoer got backstage at Coachella.

8. TRY GETTING IN DURING THE HEADLINE ACTS

It'll be pretty quiet and the security might have even nipped off to watch the music for five minutes.

9. DO SOME DUMPSTER DIVING

OK, you've got to be pretty despo for this but… is there a bin directly outside the entrance? Chances are that people leaving for the day might have chucked their lanyards in the trash so keep your eyes peeled.

10. BRACELET UP

Buy a load of cheap, sparkly glitter bracelets, the kind that every festival stall will sell, and load your wrists up with them to conceal the fact you don't have the right wristband.

11. CARRY A CHAMPAGNE GLASS

Walk in with a plastic flute like you own the place and the doormen will hopefully think you just popped out for five minutes.

12. DRESS THE PART

Think of it like the festival equivalent of trying to score an airline upgrade and dress up a little bit more than you might usually. For the girls, a black biker jacket, skinnies, and boots will do, but add red lippy and "look at me" sunnies. Boys, if you dress like that you'd probably also get in actually, as everyone will presume you're "someone."

13. MAKE FRIENDS

If you spot someone wearing the elusive VIP wristband in the crowd then what's the harm in getting to know them a little bit? It's much easier to sneak in on the arm of someone who's actually legitimately supposed to be there.

14. MAKE UP A SOB STORY

If you find a soft security guard, then a woeful tale of losing your bag/your friends/all of your family in a freak tent fire might get you in, even if it's just because they can't bear the sound of your wailing any more.

15. GET PHYSICAL

VIP areas are often separated by easily scalable fences. If you're feeling limber, work out where the security points are and take your chances with a leg up from your friend.

CHAPTER 3:
THE
PEOPLE
YOU'LL
MEET

THE PRINCESS

Fueled by pictures of Kate Bosworth wafting around Coachella in white denim cut-offs and statement jewelry, and months of "festival fashion" (more of that later) features in her fave glossy magazines, The Princess thinks of a festival in terms of its Instagrammability. As such, she has been planning the perfect lighting/backdrops/outfits/hairstyle/filters for months.

There's only one thing she's forgotten—she's going to a festival. As are thousands of other people. People who aren't Kate Bosworth. Hell, people who might not even know who Kate Bosworth is and who languish in the ignorance of not having read her 15 essential festival tips in *InStyle*. People who think they are coming along to drink booze, listen to music in a field, and pass out in tents. The imbeciles.

So, when The Princess is faced with the thousands of normal people, toilet facilities the Ministry of Defence could use for chemical warfare research, and, worst of all, a lack of electrical sockets for her straighteners/ten-speed facial cleansing brush/variety of devices used to take and subsequently upload her #festibabe albums across a minimum of four social media mediums, reality hits. Kate Bosworth doesn't actually "go" to festivals. Instead she gets flown in by helicopter, puts on her trophy jacket, and stands by a ferris wheel while someone takes her photograph. All this activity is soundtracked by the constant thrum of the Uber chopper waiting to take her back to her five-star hotel, complete with non-WMD bathrooms, restrictions on normal people, and all the electrical sockets one could dream of.

"Oh well," thinks the Princess, "maybe a little alcohol will numb the pain." Not too much booze, mind you—she can barely stomach the thought of having to pee in those torture chambers masquerading as toilets. Also, since she's been on her festival diet of 500 calories a day (a gal's gotta look good in her fringed crop top after all), any more than the recommended daily alcohol units (for a gnat, that is) will put her straight on the vomit comet. A glass of nicely chilled rosé or maybe some bubbles will do—she's definitely seen Kate Bosworth with an ice bucket of Laurent Perrier. Alternatively, if the soda water doesn't look too fizzy (she doesn't want to bloat) perhaps a couple of Skinny Bitches could be in order.

Sadly, for The Princess none of these drinks will be free. She didn't have the foresight—nor the luggage allowance—to bring in her own drink, which means her motto of "shoes before booze" doesn't sound quite so sassy as before. Instead, she'll be stuck paying the equivalent of the average hourly wage for a pint of a dubious liquid that's urine-like not only in temperature and color, but also in cloudiness and fizziness, too. Is it beer or cider? That's the question no one can quite work out.

Once the Princess gets past the revulsion of the first pint, things suddenly start to improve. The forty minutes she spent trying on different hats in her hand mirror that morning don't seem wasted, as even some of the normals around her seem to look more attractive. Why, she might even try getting a little nearer the front of the stage. This is where it all goes wrong. Once the Princess is separated from her fellow #festibabes and has to survive on her own wits she finds that those wedge wellies (so cute in the shop) are neither waterproof nor walkable. A combination of strangers' bodily fluids and spilt beer slowly soak into her pretty little socks and every step is tinged with the very real possibility of falling face first into the aforementioned fluid combination. By the time she's been swept into the middle of the crowd, her floral head garland has become snagged on the chest hair of a man she thinks might actually be high on drugs. She also has a sneaking suspicion someone might have put a cigarette out on her kimono. This brings on a full-scale meltdown, a visit to the medical tent for a "panic attack," and a $200 taxi journey back to the nearest drop-off point, where mommy and daddy will be waiting for her with clean jammies and a Valium. Next year she's doing Yacht Week.

THE DEALER

No matter how many times everyone's mother tells them to "just say no," a festival, with thousands upon thousands of willing, naïve, potential customers, is always going to be Christmas Day to a drug dealer. The Dealer, armed with an across-the-body bag stuffed full of cash and absolutely no chance of customers being able to find him again once they realize they've just paid $80 for talcum powder, LOVES festivals.

Actively searching for The Dealer? Follow the Hansel and Gretel-esque trail of nitrous-oxide canisters and resealable plastic bags the size Barbie would take her lunch to work in and you'll probably find him.

A little bit older, a lot bit sleazier, and dressed a decade behind everyone else, he will also probably be the only person in the Dance Tent not off his face.

Shiftier than a comedian from the 1970s in a sex trial, he'll be slouched by an exit, his air of studied nonchalance an instant giveaway should any police there be bothered with some bloke selling teenagers cocaine cut with so much babies' teething powder that it'd struggle to show a reading on those bleepy machines they have on *Border Force*. He will always be wearing a jacket, no matter what the temperature and will probably have a large, mute, "mate" ready to clamp down on any punters getting a bit "lively," throw in a couple of girls at least 17 times more attractive than him, prepared to pay for their highs with a quick blowie round the back, and you've found him and his crew.

Still struggling to locate him? You're going to have to try word of mouth. Gurning, dry, lock-jawed mouths will be the best source of information, if you can get a word of sense out of any of them. A word of warning though—the guy with the dreads in a rasta hat... now OK, he's definitely TV's idea of a Dealer, but in this environment he's probably the undercover cop.

THE SECURITY GUARD

No one is denying that security is essential at a festival, but forget the impressive-looking athletes you see surrounding Beyoncé or the ex-SAS hard men discretely guarding Kate Middleton. The security guys at your average festival are about as far removed from these professionals as Alexa Chung is from the dessert trolley. With the sudden need for a large number of somewhat tough men in a location where the most interesting thing that happens the rest of the year is a meat raffle, quality control of festival security is not always what it should be. Putting a hi-vis vest on a chap does not a licensed doorman make him.

As a result you need to be careful, basically. Dave might be a perfectly affable chap under that greasy-looking bomber jacket, tattooed knuckles, and skinhead, but then again he might not. He might just have been one of the only men in the surrounding area not in prison or relying on a mobility scooter and as such his able-bodiedness and ability to swerve the police are really the only reasons for his employment. Therefore, some jumped-up city kid who's paid more for his flashy new rucksack than Dave's earning in minimum wage all week is not going to do well if he gets "a bit mouthy" at the door. These Security Guards are basically St Peter to your heaven, a word from them that the dog's found something a bit suspect in your bag or that "you was looking for a fight" and that's it—you're out on your ear, no entry, no refund, no argument. So be nice to them—here's how:

1. Bite your tongue when a Security Guard confiscates that bottle of vodka that you know he'll be putting in his own bag the minute your back is turned.

2. Agree with him that the bloke in front of you was indeed dressed like a twat (quietly mind you, the aforementioned bloke in front might be pretty handy himself.)

3. If you really want to make pals/think you might need a favor from security later, then offer up a sacrifice. If you know those cans are probably going to get confiscated anyway, then why not hand the booze over before they are found. "We couldn't finish these on the train, would you boys fancy them for later?" should get them on side. Alternatively, when trawling through bags and bags belonging to "filthy bloody druggies" even the hardest of hard men appreciates a bottle of hand sanitizer. Believe us, it's got us in even when a friend had lost their wristband.

4. Get out of the way if a fight happens anywhere near you. Remember at school when you used to all crush into a corridor shouting "bundle?" Imagine that situation but with a handful of hammered festivalgoers and 15 local hard men who've been sworn at, had drinks spilt on, and have been situated dangerously near all kinds of human effluent all day. Things will get nasty.

5. On a serious note, do remember Security Guards are there to be told if something sketchy is going on. You never know, you might just appreciate Dave's particular brand of rough justice when that prick camped next to you pisses on your tent for the fourth time in a night.

THE COOL PARENTS

Booze, drugs, music at a decibel level more commonly known as "you-know-your-hearing-is-going-to-be-paying-for-this-in-30-years loud," crazies, a lack of any kind of washing or hygiene facilities, food of a nutritional level that only just allows it to be sold as safe for human consumption, a thin piece of plastic your only shelter... All these things are tough enough to cope with when you're responsible only for yourself (and maybe your friend, Dave, if he took one of those random pills he found on the floor of the Dance Tent), but what if you add a teeny, tiny little person into the mix? What if you had to look after a baby with no bladder or bowel control (not too dissimilar to Dave then) who has no concept of the sleeping patterns suitable for a festival and who wants to stick his tiny little fingers into everything and anything he sees, including that pile of regurgitated noodles containing visible, still-undigested pills of an unidentifiable nature? By bringing a kid to a festival surely you're setting yourself—and anyone within crawling/crying distance—up for a weekend of hell?

Not if you're a "Cool Parent." Broadly divided into two categories, the Hippie and the Hipster, Cool Parents have contrasting reasons for dragging their poor offspring into a field for a week. Despite these differences, they are united in their belief that it's 100 percent their "right" to do so.

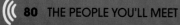

THE HIPPIES

These yoga-loving, raw-food-eating parents took their baby to Glastonbury when she was three months old. "She just slept in a hemp makeshift sling," they say—one that they paid $150 for at a world craft fair. "We wrapped her around one of us or anyone else that needed to feel the pure love of an infant." It's important to both of the Hippy Parents that baby Zen sees everyone as her mother and father, "After all, are we not all nurturing parents to this great world that we live in? It's all of our responsibilities to be mother and father to our planet, so why not also take responsibility for our babies? Festivals, much like a beautiful lake or an unspoiled field, are there for children to roam, right?"

WRONG. We'll tell you why not, Rain and Leaf (and BTW we know your real names are Ray and Lucinda)—festivals are for adults because they are full of adults. These adults are doing adult things, like swearing, having sex, and not remembering to leave dangerous objects out of the way of little fingers. And while your back is turned doing a rain dance/ boiling up someone's placenta as an afternoon snack/knitting a headdress from your own pubic hair, little Zen is at best seriously pissing off all those adults who have payed full price for their tickets, unlike your underage freeloader, and at worst seconds from drowning in a mire of mud and human filth. Leaf's parents are still hoping this hippy lifestyle is a phase and continue to pay their daughter's bills, because Rain doesn't make much money from his wooden mushroom carving business.

The grandparents have also secretly put Zen down for Eton in the hope that by the time he's six his mother will be married to a stockbroker and the nearest she'll get to a field is managing their country estate.

How to deal with them Drape yourself in animal produce and additive-filled processed food. You don't have to go the full Lady Gaga meat dress, but having a bacon sandwich more-or-less constantly in your hand and a half-empty packet of Skittles somewhere on your person that you're happy to offer to little Peace will have them relocating site quicker than an Anonymous hacker after a call from the FBI.

THE HIPSTERS

Identifiable by their four-wheel, all-terrain baby buggy that cost more than your car and their child clad in a Ramones babygro, the Hipster Parents' mantra is "why should our lives change," and they've been toting poor Arthur around to every vintage club night, cereal café opening, and AAA backstage bars since before his fontanel hardened. Such is this baby's overexposure to the hipster life that he now believes those enormous ear defenders he permanently wears—"because we're responsible parents"—are a part of his actual body. He is confused each time he sees workmen wearing them in the street and questions, "Are you my real daddy?"

The Hipster dad discovered tattoos late in life and spent a week's vacation away from his job as a conceptual architect (he does work for a lot of members clubs—more for the contacts than the cash, yeah?) getting a sleeve inked, which he now pretends took him years. The dates of birth and names of Arthur and Edna have been entwined in Roman script throughout his sleeve and he's now wondering if he can carry off an ironic neck tatt. Sadly he knows he would have to include his wife's name in the design and that wouldn't go down all that well with the 22-year-old interns he

likes to "entertain" regularly on company expenses.

The Hipster mom lost her baby weight in hours rather than weeks and only really comes to these festivals in the hope of being in a toilet queue with Kate Moss. Of course, she's also there to keep an eye on hubby and the 22-year-olds. If you're hanging with the masses, these mothers are a breed that you should be able to avoid, because they tend to exist only within the confines of the VIP area. If you are unlucky enough to encounter one, you might want to borrow her kid's ear defenders.

How to deal with them Eavesdrop on whatever conversation they're having. This shouldn't be hard, Hipster Parents like to make sure everyone can hear how fabulous they are. Once you've gathered what they are discussing, make something up around it. For example, if they're banging on about the latest secret VVIP area at the festival—a place that you have to have 47 different wristbands, GPS coordinates, and a mason's handshake to find—then make up one of your own where entry will only be guaranteed with the foreskin of an antelope and a written reference from David Guetta. They'll be trying to source those on their Apple Watches in seconds.

THE MUSIC JOURNALIST

You'd think that a free, access all areas (and bars) ticket would make most people happy. Not having to mess about being 3,748th in line on a booking website or redial the same number for four hours to hear nothing but the engaged tone is surely pretty great. The Music Journalist is not that fussed, even though her ticket turns up on a courier bike in an envelope containing enough wristbands to give her RSI and the details of the taxi that'll be taking her there.

Weighed down by years of cynicism and the fact that write-ups full of snark and sarcasm get considerably more hits than those consisting of sweetness and light, the MJ's mood depends largely on the caliber of the free bar in the VIP area and whether or not she has to use her legs to get around.

A minimal line for drinks and a full open bar that includes branded spirits, plus plentiful Wi-Fi and enough security to keep her a decent distance from the general population is the only way to make the Music Journalist resemble someone happy. A free bar you can access using only the finite amount of tokens you've been given, which serves only lager or wine and operates a less than rigorous approach to who is deemed a VIP will see the Music Journalist's temper begin to fray. A "VIP" area where regular people can come in for a mere $50 that contains a normal bar where one not only has to queue but also PAY for a drink disgusts the MJ—the organizers might as well have taken a shit in her morning espresso. As for walking, who do they think she is? A golf buggy at her beck and call (even if it is only to go and get some condoms at 4am) is the least they can do.

Once buoyed by the free booze, the Music Journalist decides she better do something with her triple-A pass and pops backstage for some gratis narcotics with the headliner. Between lines she gets three quotes from the singer that she'll later spin into a 2,000-word "color" piece. Next follows a quick trawl through the crowd, brandishing her press pass, to pick out (largely attractive) fans to give her snappy soundbites on their festival experience. If they say something good, she'll probably just nick that for herself. After that the MJ is pretty much done for the weekend and will retire back to her paid-for Winnebago. There the wordsmith will take some more of the drugs she either scored backstage or brought in (AAA wristband equals zero search at the door) and watch an hour or two of the festival on a flatscreen TV while drinking from her fridge full of the sponsor's booze and enjoying some oral delectation from one of the aforementioned attractive crowd members (he thinks he's getting a VIP wristband out of it).

The Music Journalist will emerge again early evening for her free dinner, clock that the Winnie opposite has a hot tub attached, make a mental note to ask for one of those next time, and go and have a beer next to some B-list celebs while simultaneously sneering at them and desperately hoping they'll talk to her. Then its fifteen minutes spent watching the main act before heading backstage for an exclusive afterparty, where she'll stay up all night, sleep through the entirety of the next day, and then be chauffeured driven home. Oh, and she'll have got paid for that and can claim back a week's vacation in lieu.

THE FASHION BLOGGER

Her entire motivation behind coming to a festival is to get her picture taken by "street style" photographers. With magazines and wesbites cottoning on that paying for models, makeup, lighting, and a studio costs a helluva lot more than sending some bloke with a SLR camera to a few festivals to ask pretty girls to stand like they've recently battled rickets, "street style" has become a festival phenomenon, packaged up and sold to other "rickets pose" girls as "fash inspo." If The Fashion Blogger goes home without anyone having taken her picture, the weekend will have been a failure.

Savannah has been a full-time blogger for a year. Subsisting on canapés (free and an effective diet, it's a two birds situation) and the profits from eBaying her fashion freebies, she's never actually been paid for any writing or styling. However, her elbow has been in *Vogue* China, her post on how a Breton top can literally save your life was reblogged 21 times, and she's got 11k Instagram followers, so, you know, she's right on the cusp and nothing will help push her over the edge like appearing in a festival fashion round up. Savannah knows she has to be savvy about this—one outfit a day simply will not do. What if US *Glamour* is doing a fringing piece but *InStyle* are looking for military festi-chic? The only solution is multiple, multiple outfit changes.

She starts the day trying on hats for 30 minutes in a hand mirror and panicking about how one does a top-to-toe OOTD selfie (outfit of the day for the uninitiated) without a full-length mirror. Sadly she hasn't worked out that the phone on her camera goes both ways and someone else could just take the photo, but why would anyone want to take a picture of someone or something else? Another half hour is wasted wondering whether the hashtag #festivalfashion or #festivalstyle will garner more interest—she'll obviously just do both, what harm will one more hashtag do when she's already got 47?

Next, she'll spend an hour arranging the contents of her make-up bag on a sunlit patch of grass for her first #festibeauty post. Extra effort will be given to making sure her brand-new espadrilles poke just into the frame so she can tag the pic #fromwhereIstand. After snapping her first "look of the day" with her favorite pose—the one where she tilts the side of her pelvis in a fashion that would have most doctors wondering if she was suffering from a dislocation—she'll have to ponder whether it's sunglasses on or off for outfit two. This will easily take her up to lunchtime and the problem of finding the most Instagrammable food possible. Now comes the blogger's "Sophie's choice:"
a) Do you choose the biggest, greasiest, most calorific thing you can find in order to take a cute photograph of it on its way to your mouth (never EVER let the food make its way in, obvs) for a "Hell-I-eat-what-I-want-and-I'm-still-a-size-4-don't-care vibe?"
b) Do you try to pick up some wellbeing followers and opt for a green juice and quinoa montage? By the time this quandary has been solved it's time for outfit three. Poor Sav is absolutely pooped and she hasn't even started to plan her Snapchat braid tutorial yet.

SPOT A BLOGGER

Why not amuse yourself with a fashion blogger drinking game? Take a swig of booze every time you see someone ridiculous wearing one of the following:

A hat that makes the wearer look like the man off the Quaker Oats packet

"Quirky" sunglasses

Gold body tattoos

A nose ring that you know is a clip in

Pastel-colored hair extensions

A floor-length kimono

An oversized clutch bag

A jacket where they haven't put their arms in the sleeves and have instead draped it like a cape

THE FESTIVAL VIRGIN

Weighed down like a snail by his brand new, padlocked, waterproof hiking backpack with hidden pockets for cash and valuables that would meet CIA standards, the festival first timer (or frequently his mother) has read every horror story about every festival ever and is convinced that if he does not plan for all eventualities then death is all but a certainty.

From a double pack of EpiPens (he doesn't have any allergies, but better safe than sorry for one never knows when a new medical condition could manifest itself) to 72 hours worth of dehydrated army rations (the food stalls are bound to be filthy and will charge a fortune for a ladle of gruel), the virgin has packed to survive a war zone. He has been practicing his tent erecting for three months, trying it out in all weather conditions to ensure he can get it up (stop sniggering at the back) as quickly and efficiently as an SAS officer. He's also watched Bear Grylls' entire back catalogue so that in the event of someone making off with his tent and all his belongings he can fashion a rudimentary shelter from discarded Evian bottles and forage for grubs for sustenance. This definitely happens, because his mother's cousin's hairdresser knew a first timer who had to sleep under a hedge and survive on dew for three days after everything, including the clothes he was wearing, was stolen from him while he slept.

With every second of The Virgin's time at the festival planned out with a level of flexibility that's similar to Sharia law's stance on adultery, he's printed out and laminated a schedule with a copy safely tucked in a Ziploc bag in a special pouch of his backpack and a backup hidden in a lanyard around his neck. He's knows the location of the medical and security tents and has worked out the most effective routes there, depending on weather and times of day, factoring in reasons for needing to visit them and the negative effect that say, a case of gastroenteritis or a sprained ankle may have on transit times.

Terrified by everything (again, blame the mother), his number one fear is that fellow festivalgoers will be desperate to spike his beer, so he will only drink from sealed containers that he himself has witnessed the opening of. Once it has been poured into a pint glass, he will then transfer the liquid into his own bottle with a sharply tightened lid that he will then secrete upon his person. Fear number two is unimaginable: running out of alcohol hand sanitizer. It would be tricky because he's brought a two-liter pump bottle for his tent and fourteen pocket-sized bottles (he's there for two nights), which he'll keep in the thigh pocket of his combats (another tip from Bear) with a backup attached to his can't-live-without lanyard.

After spending the first 24 hours in a state of critical panic something's gotta give. Now that may very well be The Virgin's heart, which will give up after trying to process the amount of fear-driven adrenalin being forced into its chambers, but it's far more likely that time away from mommy surrounded by every temptation one could desire he goes fully rogue and returns with a pregnant raver girlfriend, a police caution, and a misspelt neck tattoo. Good for him.

THE SUPER FAN

She arrived four days before the site even opened, because she read on a Russian fan forum* that sometimes the band liked to arrive early to perform a sound check before anyone else got there. She also showed up well in advance so that she could see the stage being erected and stand by the crowd barriers as soon as they were put up. Ain't nobody going to get in front of her, even if she does now have to wait in the same spot for 48 hours, surviving only on a diet of Pringles and obsession.

With a banner that's bigger than a removal truck proclaiming her love for each member, she knows the band will be able to spot her straight away here. That's just a precaution in case the boys—or more accurately their security team—don't recognize her from that unfortunate incident when she was found suspended six floors up trying to get into their hotel room through the window. Or the time she pretended the band's car had run over her foot in an effort to get them to stop. Or that weekend when she hid under the hospital bed of the woman having her hysterectomy next to the drummer's mother. Anyway, they'll definitely notice her here and that's all that matters.

Peeing in a bottle, being laughed at by security guards, and having to handcuff herself to the barriers to avoid the police moving her on are all minor inconveniences in the life of The Super Fan. With her five spare phone batteries in her bag, those 17-hour playlists will see her through to the moment the band arrives on stage.

Clad head to toe in fan merchandise—from the declarations of devotion inscribed across her cheeks with face paint and the "realistic" artist's impression tattoos on her arms to the limited-edition T-shirt only available on their Japanese tour ($700 on eBay)— she knows the songs better than the band themselves and could perform their stage routine with both legs tied together. She knows this because she's tried; some bitch who called herself a Super Fan challenged her on Twitter and she slayed it.

Living for the moment when the band plays the B-side of one of their lesser-known hits that was released only in Germany, she'll be in the 0.1 percentile of the crowd who has ever heard it before. A set full of hits is not what The Super Fan wants to hear, where's the devotion in that? Anyone who listens to the radio will know the hit songs. Why should these indifferent morons get to enjoy them when they don't know what a real fan is? Still, once the music starts all is well (by well it means she's sobbed her way through the first 45 minutes) until the moment the trials of the last three days catch up with her and she collapses. Right at the point she is ushered away on a stretcher by medical staff, the band choose the girl who quickly takes her place at the front to get up on stage with them.

* She learnt Russian specifically for this purpose. She doesn't know why, but Russian fans seem to have the inside scoop on this band's every move, so it really wasn't that much of a big deal to teach herself an entirely new alphabet. Not if it meant she was getting the info before those other bitches online who pretend to love them when they don't even know them, not like she does anyway.

THE MISERY

When The Misery imagined a music festival he thought of sun and fun. He looked forward to sitting on hay bales, sipping a chilled drink, and watching the sun going down while his fave band played his fave song and he had the best day of his entire summer. He hoped for cozy evenings around campfires while the girl of his dreams plays with his hair. He pictured bedding down in the great outdoors and waking to birds singing. The poor fool.

When The Misery realizes that the nearest he will get to a hay bale is the straw that someone's chucked over a pile of vomit that's too far from a source of water to be sluiced away. When he discovers that the average temperature of everything he'll drink will not be dissimilar to that of urine. When he finds out that his fave band have decided to do a set for the "real fans" and definitely won't be playing the one song that he really loves 'cos it's got too commercial and they're sick to the back teeth of it. When he sees that even the hottest human being in the world becomes physically repulsive after three days of shitting in a hole and not showering. When he accepts that waking up to the birds ain't

gonna happen 'cos YOU NEVER GET ANY FUCKING SLEEP DUE TO THE PILLHEADS CAMPED NEXT TO YOU PLAYING DRUM 'N' BASS ON THEIR BEATS BY DRE SPEAKERS ALL NIGHT, then his cheery demeanor will descend into utter despondency.

Desperate to be somewhere that's quiet, clean, dry, and away from the thousands of people all conspiring to make his life hell, the festival site soon becomes The Misery's own private version of those foreign jails you see on TV programs. The ones where drug-smuggling holiday makers are banged up for years in a terrifying South American prison, only without the comfort of someone from their native consulate fighting to free them.

All The Misery can do about his situation is WHINGE. His mates will try to cheer him up for about ten minutes and then grow sick and tired of this moaning Minnie who won't just get drunk and forget about the fact that everyone is basically living like farm animals. As a result, The Misery will retreat to the only home he has and hide in the tent. There he will eat all the cereal bars that were supposed to last him and his mates the full week of the festival. Next, he will drink and not replace all the bottled water, so no one has anything to neck the Ibuprofen with, forcing his mates to contemplate a dry swallow or a splash of contact lens solution for throat lubrication.

As the remaining three nights begin to feel like a 15-year stretch, The Misery starts weighing up his options. Leaving at this point will mean pissing his mates off and he'll have to spend a fortune on a train home because his pre-booked return ticket is only valid on the last train on a Sunday. Plus, everyone who said he wouldn't like festivals 'cos he's "just not that kind of person" would be proved right. But screw what everyone else thinks; he's going. His friends will probably die if they stay here much longer anyway.

THE BRO PACK

Never intentionally caught in a group consisting of fewer guys than it'd take to make up a couple of sports teams for an impromptu game of football (because, you know, what's life without the constant ability to break into a bout of roughhousing wherever and whenever), The Bro Pack will be initially identifiable by the unofficial bro festi-uniform.

This outfit will consist of a low-cut muscle vest with oversized armpit holes and covered with heavy branding and/or a gym-related quote along the lines of "I flexed so hard my sleeves fell off." It's worth noting that this top will be removed many times throughout the day in order to break the monotony of vest wearing and to reveal a bare chest covered in neon paint. After all, he hasn't been adding all those extra bench-press reps to keep that body under wraps. The next items of the "Bro-niform" are a baseball cap positioned at any angle other than the one it should be worn at, a pair of mid-length board shorts pulled down to a whisker away from butt-crack exposure, and some Havaianas flip-flops, especially if it's bad weather. Imagine someone dressed only in clothes stolen from the beach while the owners did a

spot of X-treme windsurfing/tandem jet skiing/go-kart kite surfing and you've got a fair idea of the look.

The Bro's main aims for the weekend are as follows:
a) To notch up as many Super-Likes as possible on his Tinder account
b) To make at least one of his mates shit himself
c) To drink alcohol only via a funnel
d) To take selfies with a variety of women in bikini tops for his social media—mainly hotties with the odd skank thrown in for total "bants."

He's aware there'll be some kind of music going on at the festival and he'll have brief look in the dance tent as he's heard that's where the girls will be wearing the least. He'll then buy some loose tea from a dealer who recognizes him for the fool he is and will spend the next two hours believing he's "fucking high man." He'll watch the evening headliner, having changed into a pair of skinny jeans and swapped his muscle vest for a Red Hot Chili Peppers T-shirt ("they're not performing but they're rock 'n' roll right, man?") that he paid $50 for from a stall that saw him coming. Of course, the ubiquitous Havaianas remain on his feet throughout.

Once ensconced in the crowd, The Bro Pack will down enough lager to sink a ship. One member will attempt to piss in a bottle—he will fail and piss all over his mate instead, who will find it hilarious. Another will snog a girl who's just vomited while his Bro will drink a pint from a stranger's Nikes—they'd use their own but a Havaiana makes a poor drinking vessel. The tallest Bro will give the shortest a wedgie so violent he could charge him the price of a vasectomy. The drunkest Bro will dance in a way that means anyone in a 5-meter radius gets all of their (and most of his) beer spilt on them before he picks the wrong guy to knock into and a fight threatens to erupt. Despite all his hours in the gym, The Bro is terrible in a fight, fearing potential damage to his good looks and the disciplinary he'll get on Monday at his law-firm internship if he has a black eye. Instead he'll opt for the "push" technique, a repeated

hand-against-chest movement that could easily be confused for a complicated courtship ritual, until the other guy swings a punch and The Pack descends en masse, dragging their boy away amidst calls of "he's not fucking worth it." Security will get involved and The Bro will inform them just what a big deal his lawyer Daddy actually is, before bursting into tears at the threat of getting a police caution and a criminal record.

THE FANCY-DRESS DOUCHE

With some festivals being almost as much about dressing up as they are booze and bands, you may need to fashion some kind of costume. For example, take Bestival, a popular festival in the UK which has a fancy-dress theme every year and if you don't make some kind of effort you'd stand out like John Mayer in a monastery. When planning your outfit there are a couple of easy-to-plunge-into pitfalls though, so give it a teeny bit of thought before you head off. Here are the most common types of fancy-dress douche you could be...

THE ONE WHO IS CULTURALLY INSENSITIVE

This sounds like an obvious one, but a plethora of celebrities and normal festival folk have in past years claimed the Native American headdress as the "perfect" festival accessory. "It just looks so cute with cut-offs and a suede crop top, right?" Wrong. "Maybe I'll even add braids for a total Pocahontas vibe." Just don't, OK. Remember, there's going to be a HUGE number of people at a festival from all walks of life. You and your mates might well have a "hilarious" in joke about a murdered pageant kid or have an entire closet of Nazi replica outfits, but if you think these "jokes" might offend someone it's best to keep them for the privacy of your own home, where there won't be any angry inebriated strangers to piss on your tent or perform an unscheduled tracheotomy with the end of their beer bottle. Oh, and as for thinking it'd be hilarious to don a wig and heels and "do" Caitlyn Jenner, it's a risky one. Shove some balloons down your khakis, draw in your cheekbones with cocoa powder, and be Kim instead, no one's going to mind you making fun out of her.

THE ONE IN YOUR GROUP WHO "FORGETS"

So you all agree on a theme and you all know it's going to really lower your attractiveness in the eyes of the opposite sex from a seven to a four, but you all also know that dressing as David Hasselhoff/Donald Trump/a seven-headed beast (all much of a muchness tbh) will be a proper laugh so you all throw yourself into it, right? Wrong. There will always be one guy or girl that accidentally on purpose forgets their "ugly" costume and just has to wear their carefully planned max-attractiveness festival wardrobe instead. He/she will pretend to be terribly bummed out that they can't join in on the fun, but sneakily will be delighted that they've upgraded themselves to an eight whenever they're stood next to you lot looking like hell.

It's not hard to deal with this trickster though. Firstly, you need to work out if you've definitely got an "accidental forgetter" in your group. Clue: it's probably the friend who put the ugliest photos of you up on Instagram because they think they look a bit like Miranda Kerr/Channing Tatum in it. Once identified, get the trickster to show you their costume just before you leave—pretend you just need to "check yours fits in." If they're really sneaky and you suspect that they might try to hurl the outfit from the car at 70 mph, claiming it was blown away by a freak windstorm in the back seat, or that they might stage a fake burglary where thieves made off with just an ill-fitting outfit but left that new iPhone next to it strangely untouched, then get together as a group and pack a backup costume— the uglier the better. The hideous outfit from the thrift store that you're 99 percent sure its previous owner died in? Perfect. The mask that was packed in the same bag as those rancid tuna sandwiches? Winner. Your forgetter will never pull that stunt on you again.

THE ONE THAT ONLY WORKS WHEN YOU'RE ALL STOOD TOGETHER

Now this is a tricky one. There are some outfits that will only work if you're all in group. For example, think of a group of country music fans deciding to get T-shirts printed with the individual letters of their favorite genre on. Now think what happens when O, R, and Y head to the bar. Make sure your outfit doesn't require you all to stick like glue to make sense.

THE ONE WHO'S GONE WAY OVER THE TOP

Suss out exactly the level of effort that all of your mates are making with their fancy dress and position yourself accordingly. If they're all fashioning homemade tinfoil hats for a space-age theme and you hire a full astronaut suit complete with breathing apparatus, you're not going to be very popular. If you're all going homemade (and it's actually a surprising amount of fun to DIY—add booze to the mix of glitter and glued-on toilet rolls and it makes for a pretty good hour or two), then not only are you going to annoy your friends by outdoing them, but you're also going to have wasted a huge amount of money that could be better spent on booze and having fun when you're there. Plus, you'll also either be so paranoid about your cost-a-fortune outfit that you'll panic anytime anyone gets so much as a splash of mud/urine/black Sambuca (believe us you'll be covered in the lot before the festival is over) near you or you'll forget you put down a week's wages as a deposit at the costume hire shop and get a nasty shock when you return it covered in crap.

It's also worth remembering that YOU HAVE TO CARRY YOUR COSTUME. So even if you didn't spend a penny on that cereal box Transformer robot costume, the three extra bags you're going to have to transport it in are going to be a right pain in the ass.

THE ONE WHO LETS THE SIDE DOWN

Whereas you have no desire to be the dick who shows everyone up, neither should you be the dick who lets everyone down. If your group are all going for a pink color theme, don't think that one pair of socks tinted pink from going in the wash with a red T-shirt are gonna cut it. Likewise, parting your hair in a slightly different way will not get you off the hook if you're all doing 70s. Make an effort, hey?

THE ONE WHO FORGETS ABOUT THE WEATHER

This isn't like the fancy-dress party you went to as Hulk Hogan when you were seven and your parents had to come and get you because some bigger boys said your bandana was shit. Once you leave your tent and trek to the site in your outfit it's one hell of a hassle to go back and get changed because you haven't factored in the weather. You might think this would apply most strongly to being underdressed when the rain starts hammering it down, but that's the lesser of two evils. In this case you just fork out for an overpriced poncho or pinch a hoodie. However, if you thought it'd be a great idea to dress in a full dinosaur outfit complete with furry head and the sun decides to put in an appearance, then you, my friend, are screwed and heatstroke is imminent.

THE ONE WHO WEARS A MANKINI

Come on guys, Borat was like 15 effing years ago, and even then wearing a mankini wasn't particularly funny. The same goes for any costume that flashes too much flesh. Remember, all that exposed skin hasn't seen so much as a flannel for 72 hours and no one wants it all up in their grill.

THE ONE YOU CAN'T USE THE BATHROOM IN

We refer you back to the onesie discussion on page 32. If your outfit means you have to get naked to pee, then it's a no.

THE CRUSTY

Never knowingly under tie-dyed, the main lure of the festival for The Crusty is the freedom to wallow in his own muck and mire, free from the criticism and judgment of others. This is the only time that he (for it is often the male of the species that falls prey to this stereotype) finds everyone has been brought down to his level of personal hygiene.

The Crusty calls himself Spyder and insists that the Y is terribly important. After all, why the hell should he spell it with an "I" just because "the Man" wants him to? He has been going to music festivals since the days of the "real festivals," which consisted of naked longhaired men on stage playing sitar to other naked longhaired men. These parties had none of the ridiculous modern-day fripperies of medical tents and designated toilets. "Those were the days."

Spyder is sad to admit that recently the nudity has taken a backseat—after his triple bypass operation he found a cold can really set him back so getting his kit of is not worth the risk. Instead he's replaced bare flesh with clothes made from fabrics usually reserved for transporting animal feed, and he tops off this look with an embroidered Fez-like hat that has fused to his fledgling dreadlocks.

Deaf in one ear and with just 30 percent hearing in the other thanks to an unfortunate incident in '78 when three days of LSD led him to believe a 50,000-watt speaker was a feather bed, it's no longer about the music for The Crusty, the vibe is the key. A field and poor sanitation are Spyder's version of utopia. He doesn't differentiate between living that way because he's chained to the foundations of a to-be-demolished building to protect a rare sub-species of toad once spotted 5 miles away, or paying $150 for the privilege.

LSD and an almost permanently attached roll-up cigarette have been usurped by legal highs and a joss-stick flavored e-cigarette (the triple bypass rears its head again) but one thing remains the same—his dance moves. These occupy a position somewhere between a man on fire attempting to extinguish himself using only the power of his arm movements and a duck caught in quicksand. The undulations of The Crusty's body belie both his age and normal human joint movement. Upon spotting an example of this breed it's advisable to remain at least three meters away at all times. That way you will not only keep your nasal hairs intact and your sense of smell in one piece, but also avoid spilling your beer when a vigorous elbow jerk dance movement thrusts your cup up into your face.

THE GROUPIE

Stacey is an eight. No, not size eight, durrrr—what do you think she is, some kind of heifer? She's a size two, obv, apart from the terrible month when that fugly bitch at Starbucks messed with her morning almond milk vanilla latte. The Starbitch switched in full-fat milk after Stacey complained to the manager that the server's acne was totally ruining her post-Spinning with Mindfulness class morning positivity. A whole 20 cups of disgusting fat-laden cow mucus passed Stacey's lips before she caught the server red-handed. Nothing non-organic had made its way into Stacey's body (and yes guys, semen is totally organic, even if it does come via a steroided-up football hero) since 2009, so the milk was kind of a big deal AND it swelled her up to almost a size 4.

That incident ruined a whole three days of her summer vacay before Stacey was able to shed those 2.5 pounds with a touch of recreational laxative abuse. The weight had to go, because everyone knows fat girls have to buy their own mimosas.

Anyway, Stacey is an eight—as in two off a ten. In the right light and right Instagram filter she's been known to be a nine, FYI. Recently, she's moved on from dating college football players and turned her attention to trying to sleep with real stars. To do this, Stacey has realized there's no better hunting ground for a rock-star boyfriend than a festival. In order to improve her chances of snaring a lead singer, she's put in the hours. Firstly, there were the gym workouts designed to ensure her buttocks are the perfect on-the-go serving platter for any rock star's class As. Next was the repeated pausing and rewinding of MTV's Top 50 Festival Anthems so that she could familiarize herself with the musicians who don't stand at the front with the microphone and haven't been seen out on a date with Katy Perry. Most important were the evenings spent bestowing "favors" on the roadies, sound engineers, assistants, friends of security guards, and third cousins, twice removed of potential headline acts.

Having now completed her training, Stacey can't quite decide whether the prize of being the one to go backstage is enough, or whether to play the long game of trying to get knocked up by a band member. She's weighed up the positives and negatives for getting pregnant:

PROS: child maintenance, a minimum nine months of fame, the kid will probably be good looking.*

CONS: fat ass, possible ruined vagina, maternity wear.

Whatever she decides, it'll make for a few killer Instagram posts.

*provided the baby's father is not a drummer—why are they never hot?

THE EARLY DOORS CASUALTY

Nothing gets a party started like a little pre-gaming, hey? And en route to a festival is the perfect time to warm up a little with a couple of pre-party liveners. A few cocktails in a can on the train down, the best part of a four pack on the bus, a bottle of wine straw-pedoed in the queue... Hang on a minute, you might think you're doing the right thing by getting 90 percent tanked up on booze you don't have to pay festival prices for, but be wary of becoming The Early Doors Casualty. It's a fine line between being a savvy boozer and the person every other festivalgoer takes a photo of to vomit shame on social media. This phenomenon is not just limited to first-day nerves either. Once ensconced in the festival site, the acceptability of having an alcoholic drink in your hand at any time of the day or night can go to some people's head. This basically results in the EDC paying the equivalent of a month's wages for the privilege of passing out while people laugh at him/her.

There will probably be at least one Early Doors Casualty in your group and it might be you. If you want to avoid a pre-lunchtime spate of unconsciousness or need to deal with someone in the grips of EDC, do read on…

1. IT CAN BE WHAT YOU DRINK, NOT HOW MUCH

"But I only had wine, the others had beers and drank loads more than me." So goes the plaintive cry of the girl who thought she was being classy by necking a bottle and a half of "2-4-1" bargain basement Chardonnay pre-11am. The lesson here is that wine is not a breakfast drink. If you want something with your cornflakes, choose a drink that's a bit more AM appropriate, such as lager.

2. EAT SOMETHING

Shovel some carbohydrates—as many as you can fit down your throat—before, after, and during boozing. Now is definitely not the time to be sticking to any kind of diet, so feel free to gorge on all the fries, bread, noodles, and pasta you can manage. You need stodgy absorbance to enable all-day boozing and help you make it through to the encore of the headline act.

3. GET SOME WATER DOWN YOU

Has your pee turned to syrup? Then you're dangerously close to EDC. Get glugging some H_2O. Try to drink a glass for every alcoholic drink you have—you will forget but if you do it 60 percent of the time then you're onto a winner.

4. DON'T FEAR THE VOMIT

Sometimes a tactical puke is the only thing that will bring you back from the brink. Take yourself off for a quiet few minutes and do it while you're still in control of your esophagus, in a location where you can retain a bit of dignity.

5. TRY A POWER NAP

Feeling woozy? An hour back in your sleeping bag can work wonders. If it's the middle of the day it'll be the closest you get to some peace and quiet, too.

6. IGNORE THE TEARS

An oft-repeated stage of an incoming EDC crisis, especially with—but not exclusive to—women, is the unexplained tears. Now, tempting as it might be to fling your arms around your poor mate as she sobs uncontrollably at a song that just "really, really fucking means something, I mean really," you're really better off pretending it's not happening. Let her sit down for a quiet few minutes then distract her with something and hopefully you'll be able to ride this stage out.

7. DON'T BE MEAN

Tempting as it is to take a photograph of your EDC friend with a very suspicious stain over his crotch and strands of vomit decorating his jumper, don't be a dick and put it on Facebook. We've all been there.

THE BACHELORETTE PARTY

Getting together a group of girls who don't know and/or don't like each other (tick as applicable) to do an activity that costs a fortune and that they'd never dream of doing in any situation where they can exercise free will is tricky. It's bad enough when that activity is an afternoon sewing the wedding logo (entwined initials of the B and G, obvs) onto underwear. It's even worse being made to have a creepy dual massage with the weird colleague at the municipal swimming pool with a room out the back doing "spa" treatments, or having to learn how to lap dance on a tandem. But these activities pale into insignificance when you are made to go on a festival hen do or bachelorette party.

Die-hard festival fans will hate the fact that they're going with a bunch of amateurs who won't know the exact ratio of ketamine to vodka Red Bull consumption needed to ensure the perfect night. The cool girls will be mortified that their Kate-Moss inspired, carefully planned look is ruined by being made to wear a "Claire's Festive Festival Fillies" T-shirt. The mothers will fret about how to manage a hot flush in a tent. The festival virgins will spend months working themselves into a frenzy over the toilet facilities before taking so much Imodium the night before that they won't defecate again until the day of the actual wedding. Everyone else will be furious that they've got to spend quite so much money and time on someone they don't even like that much.

Lay the blame at the door of the Maid of Honor who, as a cover story, claims the bride thinks spa weekends and drinking posh cocktails in a nice bar are "boring." In reality she just worked out that she could scam a free ticket herself by the time she'd overcharged the rest of the group for "dressing up bits" and "fizz" (the cheapest sparkling wine on offer). She'll spend $10 a head on the aforementioned T-shirts, getting them all made in a small because that's her size and it was cheaper and easier to get them as a job lot in the same size. Next, she'll buy some inflatable penises to stick to the tent of the bride, and splash out on a fake veil so flammable that someone is guaranteed third-degree burns by the end of the weekend. This leaves her with enough cash leftover for her own ticket and a massive wedge of cash for spending money.

The weekend will pan out with one group falling out because one of the girls couldn't stick to the "Sistas B4 Mistas" rule and shagged some guy on one of the other girl's brand-new floral-print sleeping bag. By the end of day one at least 50 percent of the group will be in in tears because:

a) Their phone ran out of battery and they have never not said goodnight to *insert name of loser boyfriend* for the whole three years they've been together.

b) They heard one of the others throwing shade at their fringed kimono.

c) They drank too much vodka.

d) They had to be the sensible one sluicing vomit off the chin of the bride's recently divorced cousin who "doesn't usually drink."

e) They had to be the poor sap to pull up the knickers of a never-met-before college friend who decided this was the perfect weekend to try drugs for the first time.

f) They had to make repeated trips to the police tent to report missing phones/handbags/virginities that the "victims" then find in their handbag/tent/pocket.

The bride will then get so fed up with everyone else that she'll head off on her own and end up having a tent quickie with a man where the only rubber involved being that on his Hunter wellies, thus inducing three weeks of period paranoia. Still, all that worry means at least she'll be able to fit into the dress no problem.

THE GLAMPERS

Now glamping has attracted somewhat of a bad rep over the last few years. Surely this is in no small way down to the very word. Fashion loves a ridiculous portmanteau and this toe-curlingly cringey fusion of glamour and camping is one of its worst, summoning up images of subtly highlighted yummy mummies serving Boden-clad children kale chips on a rug made from the wool of sheep they helped shear on a sustainability-focused wellness retreat, while Daddy takes an important business call arranging to sell a little-known African country in the background. OK, we're not going to lie to you... that is pretty much exactly what glamping is like—everyone is rich, everyone is clean. Most of them are dicks but if you get the chance to do it, then do. Here's why (and some ideas for other things to call it so you don't sound like the kind of prick that says "I'm off glamping"):

1. YOU GET BETTER CAR PARKING

No parking seven miles away and lugging your crate of beer through 15 acres of swampy farmland. There will be a special super-close car park for you exclusive glampers and if it's too far away they might even provide valet parking.

2. YOU DON'T HAVE TO WALK. ANYWHERE

If you've never experienced the delights of being driven around everywhere you want to go (and we mean everywhere) in a golf buggy, then for that reason alone you should try glamping. We can't guarantee you'll get one at every festival but a lot of them do have a team of whizzy little vehicles ferrying anyone too tired/hammered/lazy/phobic of mixing with non-glamping folk anywhere they want to go. You don't know the true meaning of the word "smug" until one of these buggies drives you safely (and dryly)

through doors closed to 95 percent of the festival crowd.

3. YOU PROBABLY WON'T HAVE TO STAY IN A TENT (AND IF YOU DO, YOU DEFINITELY WON'T HAVE TO PUT IT UP)

When is a tent not a tent? When it's a luxury yurt complete with wood-burning stove, 1,000-thread-count Egyptian cotton bedsheets, and a four-person hot tub. Whereas this is at the highest extreme of the glamping scale, you'll find that alternative glamping accommodation such as pod pads (little shed-like things,) Winnebagos, camper vans, gypsy caravans, and upcycled milk floats all provide a very comfortable night's sleep. Even if it's an actual tent (quelle horreur!), there will be some nice bloke called Dave to put it up for you and make sure your air beds are fully inflated.

4. THERE WILL BE SHOWERS!

And clean(ish) toilets—the rich banker boys who can afford to do this have no better control over their urine stream or cocaine-addled bowels than any other festivalgoers we're afraid. But these portable toilets will be posh with bowls of potpourri and constantly replenished toilet rolls. Yes, the showers will be a bit "high school locker room," but still of a better caliber than that last AirBnB you stayed in.

5. IT'S THE ULTIMATE CHAT-UP LINE

Who isn't going to want to bed down with you in luxury rather than return to a mildewed tent and be forced to kip top to toe with Big Dave and his athlete's foot. Let the news of your superior sleeping arrangements spread throughout the crowd and you'll be inundated with offers.

6. THEY DON'T SEARCH YOU AS RIGOROUSLY

Now don't take this as gospel as you might be the unlucky sod who gets their extra bottle of cough syrup and that half carafe of Châteauneuf-du-Pape confiscated, but as a general rule security are a little more lax with their "special" guests—which can also make smuggling your contraband new buddy in for the night (see above) rather easier.

7. YOU'LL PROBABLY HAVE A CELEBRITY NEIGHBOR

Find yourself shacked up next to One Direction's tour bus (this genuinely happened to me) and you'll make the price of your ticket back selling stories about the regularity of their energy drink consumption and the frequency of visits from members of the opposite sex. If you're not quite that mercenary, it'll still be an opp for a good few selfies for social, hey?

8. THE TICKETS DON'T SELL OUT AS QUICKLY

Even at sold-out events the glamping tickets are often still available, as the majority of festivalgoers don't want to fork out. So if you're despo to go, glamping could be a good option.

9. YOU'LL HAVE ELECTRICITY

This provides you with the rarest of commodities at a festival: a smart phone that never dies. If you're feeling entrepreneurial you could even charge people to charge.

10. OK, YOU'VE CONVINCED ME, BUT WHAT THE HELL ELSE CAN I CALL IT?

Let's stick with the portmanteau theme and see what else we can come up with:

Lamping: Lazy camping
Spenting: Special tenting
Yumping: Yuppie camping
Pomping: Posh camping
Examping: Expensive camping

No, they all sound just as shit. Sorry. You're just going to have to deal with it.

CHAPTER 4:
BEWARE

FESTIVAL HORROR STORIES

If you take nothing else from this book, please read the following horror stories. Having said that, perhaps not while you're eating or if you're feeling a little sensitive, because they are largely bathroom based. Sorry.

THE GIRL WHO DROPPED HER PHONE DOWN THE TOILET (AND FOLLOWED IT IN)

Immortalized in the UK tabloid newspapers as "Poo Girl," one 18-year-old festivalgoer got stuck headfirst in a portable toilet at Britain's Leeds Festival.

Having had her bag with all her money and valuables stolen from her tent at the festival the year before, poor Charlotte Taylor decided she'd go for the sensible option of carrying all her cash, along with her return train ticket and phone in her bag at all times. So far, so good—until the unthinkable happened.

Having answered the call of nature, Charlotte turned to exit the toilet, but her bag slipped off her shoulder and fell down into the bowl. It's worth noting that this was lunchtime of her first day there, so by this stage she hadn't even seen a single band and had no booze inside her to blame for dropping the bag or to numb her from the pain that was about to ensue. Faced with seeing her entire weekend go, literally, down the toilet, she panicked and did the only thing she could think of—dive in after her belongings.

When Charlotte couldn't reach her bag with one hand, she tried using both arms, reaching deeper into the toilet until she was up to her shoulders. Now, if you haven't already, take a minute to think where her face would be at this point and try not to vomit. Unfortunately, as Charlotte struggled to reach down to grasp the bag (which was covered in exactly what you'd imagine), she suddenly got wedged stuck. Now, if you've ever been physically stuck in anything—from a too-tight dress, where you're seconds away from Incredible Hulking it off, to trying on a friend's ring then realizing you've actually cut off all blood supply and begin to wonder how much you really need that finger anyway—you'll know that the first thing you do is panic. As Charlotte

struggled more things got even worse, but thankfully after 20 minutes her friend came looking for her, sensing that even that dodgy breakfast burrito couldn't have detained her for that long. The friend raised the alarm with the fire brigade who at first didn't believe the story (would you?). Eventually the firemen were convinced and went to the toilet, where they discovered the immobile Charlotte. They then proceeded to take the roof off the cubicle and, after much pulling from above, managed to free her.

Charlotte was then promptly marched to the showers. Here festival staff hosed her down and dressed her in clothes from the welfare tent (think of the indignity of having to wear clothes from the "lost and found" at school, but multiplied by 1,000). If that wasn't enough trauma, rumor of her ordeal spread, making her the laughing stock of the whole festival for the rest of the weekend.

THE MAN WHO CLIMBED INTO THE TOILET LOOKING FOR DRUGS

Remember the scene in the movie *Trainspotting* where Ewan McGregor loses his opium suppositories in the "Worst Toilet in Scotland" and ends up swimming through rivers of diarrhea in search of his lost drugs? Well, one man thought this wasn't so much an exploration of the depths of depravity that addicts would sink to, but instead a really great way of nabbing yourself some free drugs at a festival.

It happened at a festival in Oregon, when an unnamed man (well, wouldn't you want to remain nameless, too?) had to be rescued by police after climbing down into the pit below the portable toilets searching for any shitted-out drugs that orifice-smuggling attendees might have been remiss enough not to catch first. Don't believe it? There is a picture on the internet if you're brave enough to google it.

THE PERVERT

Can you imagine how desperate for a flash of genitals you'd have to be to consider secreting yourself in the depths of a toilet pit? This happened at a yoga festival in Colarado when a woman lifted the loo seat to find a man hiding there. There are two serious issues with this:

a) Who the hell goes to a yoga festival anyway? Green juice and sitting in the lotus position for eight hours a day doesn't sound like fun.

b) Going back to that green juice, can you imagine what the collective waste of people subsisting on wheatgrass shots and quinoa is like. Eww.

The pervert fled the scene but was later arrested—he wasn't exactly hard to track down, covered as he was in fecal matter. Although he denied the charges, he subsequently gave an interview to a newspaper where he said he felt the women's excretions were blessing him, saying, "I was doing a little bit of yoga, and I'm just seeing all these goddesses. It seems crazy, but I just felt like I was being blessed by their energy."

When questioned about the health issue, he remained unperturbed, stating, "There's bacteria in there, but to me it's just normal... we all have bodily fluids. I still would have done it even if it smelled a little weird, because where there is muck, there is gold."

Surely there's a club night for this kind of thing?

THE TIME SOMEONE GOT BLOW AND SUCK MIXED UP

We'll presume the sewage-gathering machine at Glastonbury that covered the Dance Tent in its contents when it was instead supposed to be sucking up the mud was merely operated by a teenage girl who hadn't yet received a reply to her anonymous letter to *Seventeen* magazine's Agony Aunt inquiring after the realities of giving oral sex. "I mean, it's called a blow job, but am I supposed to suck?"

The machine was appropriated from its usual toilet-sucking duties to scoop up the quagmires of mud that threatened to engulf the festival in 1998 following a period of particularly heavy rain. Instead, the organizers were forced to close down a section of the tent after the vehicle spluttered gallons of effluent from floor to ceiling.

THE GIRL WHO FELL ASLEEP IN A SEWAGE SLIPSTREAM

It's a familiar enough story—you drink a bit (far) too much, the sun is a bit too hot (it's 100 degrees and you haven't drunk any water in 48 hours), you really want a snooze (OK, more like a blackout/partial coma), and your tent is oh-so-far away. What to do? Find a quiet-ish corner of the field and settle yourself down for 40 winks, of course.

Easier said than done. With the available space-to-person ratio at a festival being not entirely dissimilar to that which you encounter on a packed commuter train, the chances of finding somewhere nice to lie down where you won't be stomped on by inconsiderate revellers are slim. This was exactly the thought process of one girl at Glastonbury festival in 2008. Having overdone things a little, she wandered (staggered) off in search of somewhere she could get a little peace (pass out) and thought she'd hit the jackpot when she found a secluded little patch of grass at the bottom of a small hill. So far, so good.

Unfortunately, her 20-minute nap lasted rather longer than intended and during this period of unconsciousness the toilets at the top of the hill (a detail she'd missed) became flooded and because gravity rarely cuts anyone a break, their contents had run down the hill, straight into her snooze spot. So deep into her sleep was she that even this river of effluent didn't rouse her and she slumbered on in her bed of mire until her friends, having been searching for her for over an hour, finally found her. Understandably horrified that their friend had basically just taken a full body shower in shit, they tried their best to rinse her off using their $6 bottles of Evian and thought they'd done an OK job.

Fastforward six months and the girl suddenly starts losing clumps of her hair. After toing and froing to the doctors finds out that the side that's suffering was the same side that she was laying on during the poomageddon incident and that despite their best efforts, that light sluicing with the Evian still left quite a bit of fecal bacteria hanging round her scalp, which caused a pretty nasty infection. The moral of the story? If you can smell the toilets, you're definitely too near to nap.

THE CRAZE FOR PORTA-TIPPING

Remember Jackass, that "hilarious" early noughties gang who'd throw dog bones onto each other's scrotums or create a merkin out of angry bees? Well we blame them for this one as they were the first to show the world the concept of portapotty-tipping. Yep, it's exactly as it sounds—wait until your friend is firmly ensconced in a portable toilet, barricade the door shut, and then tip it over, thus creating an inescapable chamber of human filth.

The Jackass crew named the prank the "poo cocktail" and it was the first official Jackass stunt. The boys used a truck to tip a toilet containing cast member Johnny Knoxville a full one-eighty degrees in order to cause maximum spillage, but since then resourceful pranksters have realized that no machinery is necessary. Festivalgoing meatheads have worked out that if two or three of them are drunk enough to ignore the fact that they'll probably dislocate their shoulders and the portable toilet happens to be positioned on a slight slope, then they can shove into a toilet ram-raid style with a force that should be more than enough to turn it on its side. This exact thing happened to one man at a British festival, who miraculously escaped with no physical injuries but who suffered panic attacks and flashbacks afterwards. Definitely not cool guys.

FESTIVAL HORROR STORIES **123**

STAYING SAFE

If you read nothing else in this book (because your parents bought it for you on Amazon in a mad panic that their precious baby is going to get murdered/impregnated/sold into modern slavery on his/her first festival trip and you think you're way too cool to need a book to tell you what to do), please pay a little attention to this entry. This section is basically going to explain how not to die and/or get into a situation that means you need to leave/get ejected from the festival when you've barely had time to enjoy yourself.

LOOK AFTER YOUR DRINK

Drink spiking isn't some made-up fairy tale. Yes, everyone's heard those urban myths about someone getting spiked and waking up naked at an airport in Germany, or thinking they were Michael Caine for 48 hours, but sadly it does happen at festivals. Some people are looking for easy targets to rob, or worse, and some assholes just think it's funny to see what happens when they get someone unknowingly wasted. Avoid putting your drink down on the floor when you dance (you shouldn't do this anyway because you're likely to spill it and at these prices that's gonna be painful), get a friend to hold it when you go to the toilet (do not attempt to take it with you—where exactly on that fetid floor do you think you're going to rest it while you do your business?), and don't hand it over to anyone you've only just met. If you do suspect something has happened, tell a member of security immediately.

BE SENSIBLE ABOUT DRUGS

Obviously the safest thing to do with drugs is to avoid them, but we need to be realistic. People are always going to take drugs at festivals and if you're going to be one of them then doing it as safely as you can is important.

Do Bear in mind that they are illegal and if you get caught with them you'll at best have them confiscated and at worst be ejected from the site or arrested. Do you want to run that risk?

Don't Use a festival to try a drug for the first time. You'll have no idea how your body will react and no one wants to be the person fitting and shitting in the middle of a 100,000-strong crowd.

Do Remember that drugs will affect your judgment, so stick with your friends and don't wander off on your own.

Don't Think you can trust that you're getting what you think you're paying for. If that sketchy guy in the corner tried to sell you a Rolex you probably wouldn't go for it, right?

Do Keep glugging that water. Acquaint yourself with the free water stations and visit them. A lot.

CROWD SAFETY

Whoever said there's safety in numbers had obviously never been at the front of a 60,000-person crowd at a festival when the headline act comes on. As tempting as a front-row seat* is, the epicenter of a drunk, excitable crowd can be a pretty scary place and people often get hurt. The other problem with being at the front is you are essentially trapped in position by thousands of bodies. Aside from the risk of being crushed, that also means no peeing, no moving to get extra food or drink, and nowhere to escape to when the other people also trapped behind you start pissing (and worse) into bottles and lobbing them into the crowd. To be honest, the atmosphere at the edges of the crowd is often way better. You'll have room to dance and won't give yourself a bladder infection by holding in three pints of lager for four hours.

*for seat, read "less than three inches square of standing room"

As a separate note, crowd surfing rarely ends well. From getting pickpocketed by opportunist thieves to being groped and prodded by opportunist perverts, there's not a lot going for it. The worst outcome of crowd surfing? When everyone forgets to hold you up causing you to fall and dislocate things you didn't even know you owned.

WATCH OUT FOR BAD DRUNKS

Remember that booze doesn't make everyone a happy ray of sunshine and that massive quantities of alcohol turn some people into aggressive dicks. Drink-fuelled fights are inevitable at festivals and, just like a brawl in a busy bar, they can soon involve a huge crowd. If you see something kicking off it's best to move away, even if you have just nabbed your dream viewing spot. After all, you're not going to be able to see very well through two black eyes. Also, keep an eye on your own aggression. Yes, it's annoying when someone spills their drink on you or steps on your foot, but it's a festival not a tea dance. These things happen so relax and don't snap.

SEX

We don't have to tell you to bag it up do we? If you haven't brought your own, then the medical tent will have some to give out.

DON'T BE AFRAID TO "TELL TALES"

If you see something that looks a bit dodgy or dangerous, don't be worried about telling the on site staff. It's what they're there for.

INDEX